Island $

C0000232663

Mother Mary Agnes, of the diocese of Aberdeen and Orkney, was born in Nottingham and spent her early years in a small mining village, the daughter of a fitter's mate and his handicapped wife. At an early age she was influenced by the life of Francis of Assisi, and also by the more spartan spirit of the Celtic Church. An introduction to Scotland added a touch of magic. All these, and the tragic early death of a much-loved mother, drew her inevitably towards the fulfilment of the religious life. After more than 20 years as a Franciscan Sister in Devon she began a new religious life as a solitary on the remote island of Fetlar in Shetland. Here, she has been joined by other women seeking the same solitary lifestyle and subsequently has founded The Society of Our Lady of the Isles (SOLI).

Also by Mother Mary Agnes and published by SPCK:

A TIDE THAT SINGS
THE SONG OF THE LARK

Island Song

Mother Mary Agnes, SOLI

With illustrations by the author

Published in Great Britain in 2001 by
SPCK
Holy Trinity Church
Marylebone Road
London NW1 4DU

Copyright © SOLI 2001

Second impression 2003

All rights reserved. No part of this book may be reproduced or
transmitted in any form or by any means, electronic or mechanical,
including photocopying, recording, or by any information storage
and retrieval system, without permission in writing from the
publisher.

British Library Cataloguing-in-Publication Data

A catalogue record for this book is available from
the British Library

ISBN 0-281-05391-X

Typeset by
Pioneer Associates, Perthshire
Printed and bound in Great Britain by
Antony Rowe Ltd., Chippenham, Wiltshire

To my sister, Carole, with love
and thanks

Contents

*With deepest love and thanks
to each member of my SOLI family for their
loving support and help to me while
writing this book.*

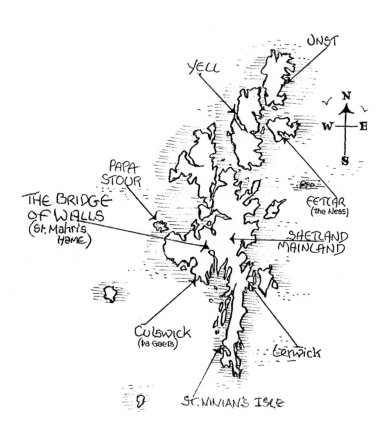

UNST

YELL

PAPA STOUR

THE BRIDGE OF WALLS
(St. Mahri's Hame)

FETLAR
(The Ness)

SHETLAND MAINLAND

Culswick
(Da Gaers)

Gerwick

St. NINIAN'S ISLE

N
W — E
S

Prologue

Burying my head into the pillow and tugging the duvet higher over my recumbent form, I prayed, prayed that soon, very soon, dear God, the storm would be stilled. Yet, the hurricane's horny fingers tirelessly fretted away trying to force entrance, its wrath spewing torrents of cascading rain down the roof before whirling it into the ocean. I pressed the pillow further into my ears to muffle the sound, though only to release my hold a few moments later to listen anew. Every joint of the timber-clad house strained against the elements.

A gentle movement made me pull an arm from under the bedclothes and reach out to touch a soft, silky head. It was Flugga, now a fragile, elderly puss. He repositioned himself against my legs and I could feel the vibration of a sudden purr as he, in turn, stretched a long front leg across my arm and flexed his paw. Crack! Another gale-force gust jolted the bed. The skylight above us seemed the main target of battle and the storm-fiend, ceaselessly slating his fury against it, shook out the very guts of the pane, rattling, rattling, determined to break every resistance . . . he scored! The large rectangular light lifted, but just as quickly clapped back into place, though not before allowing a streak of cold air to sizzle across the room. Rattle, rattle, once more the pane was prised ajar and this time a wet draught hissed past my face. Groping a hand across a bedside chest-of-drawers, I snatched up a torch, and again the window, thankfully, sank into its frame.

Now, hardly allowing myself to breathe, I stiffened, waiting, ready for the next violent onslaught. Was it taking longer to come? One second, two, three . . . Boom! Again, the whole canopy of heaven erupted, fragmenting the air around me, and shredding the last ounces of the sense of security that this small room had given.

I sat up abruptly. Could the frail little cat hear the rumpus or feel the turbulence? If he could, he showed no signs of anxiety. Of course, living at the centre of his own tiny world and warm against my legs, he was content.

Through the dark turmoil of the storm the world continued to crash around us, and yet soon, despite the mayhem, a warmth from the centre of my own being stirred, enabling me to plunge below all the outer terrors of the night to a place of hope. Here, I longed to drop into quietness, to drop into the peace of Christ. I waited . . . though my uneasiness did not pass, but only changed and moved into a new divergence of itself. With its stretch and with its tension it moved into the 'contention' of trying to understand and interpret, into the strife of that which pulls out meaning for others. Now it was a battle of love, and willingly I wrestled with the wind and the waves of life. I tore at the tempests of mind and soul, in order to pull out truth, the truth for me and the truth for all God's people. I strained, toiling, labouring and grappling to put meaning into words, simple words. To pull out words, words . . . yet how could mere words be sufficient? How could any words ever explain the wonder of what lay beneath the raging of the world? How could they, words, explain the Infinite, or that place where, he, the Absolute, dwells? Could strung together, man-made sentences pour meaning across the universe or pour out the meaning of him who, himself, is the eternal, incarnate Word? Could any paragraph, chapter or book, unveil or ever utter knowledge of him, the living God, or divulge the mystery of that sacred lodging, that location, that holy temple, that deep, precious habitation which is called the human heart and where he, eternal Love, longs to abide? No, never can a human word declare these things. At least never can a human word that is not the Christ himself, reveal how glorious that centre of being is, that centre so firmly located within each one of us, within each creature and within every beloved child of the Father.

Clang! Clash! Hammer, knock, hammer, hammer, hammer . . . ferociously the skylight shuddered once more, snapping open its jowls; but again, thank God, it slammed shut. 'Oh, please hold out until morning,' I begged, 'and I promise, I'll invent a really tight fastening to hold you down for the rest of the winter.' I spun the soft beam of my torch across the lurching window and then cast it in Flugga's direction. No, he struggled with nothing that life hurled at him.

Sliding under the bedclothes again, I returned anew to my thoughts, allowing my heart to reflect on its own, constant ache to tell the world, and all those who knew nothing of their heritage, of the glory. To tell the whole earth about that tiny heart-room which lies within each one of us, to tell everyone about our incredible inheritance of heaven and of peace . . . peace . . . If only nations could be aware of this place, of this place that is so tiny and yet so vast, aware of this heaven in the heart. If only God's children themselves could be aware of this pool of the deepest stillness, constantly rippling into song, into a singing tide, into the freedom of a wide blue sky and bird wings, then into song again, a song that throbs from the tiniest throat of a lark. Dear God, how I longed to show them so that they too could sing, show them, that within their own precious beings they possess heaven on earth and that the whole earth sings and that its song is the song of Love, the song of God himself. How such yearning hurts, such glimpses into the human heart . . . this heart, where wisdom and simplicity embrace and all recognition and knowledge of beauty lie beyond words. This heart, this place of perfection, where abides, so homely, the great mystery of light and of truth, the great mystery of the creator himself, the Christ. Letting go of self I turned to receive him.

The storm still spat out its fury, but it no longer mattered. Nothing mattered, least of all a storm, for storms can only rattle and thunder around the circumference of our lives in this world. No turbulence can ever touch that deep well at the centre of our beings unless we ourselves allow it to do so. Nothing can touch us, God's little ones, if we are in that place of communion in him. Held by him, in the chalice of the heart, the chalice into which we have had the courage to plunge, divested of all the superfluous trappings of body, mind and spirit in order, to abide in him. No, nothing can ever harm us there, for that is the abode where the King in his beauty unites us with himself, in an unspeakable communion of love.

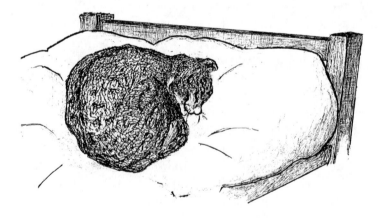

I watched Flugga, who is not one to miss an opportunity, totter unsteadily up the bed and then without nonsense and for such an 'old boy', deftly and neatly, curl in the crook of my nearest arm. That was nice, for now I could actually hear his purring, music indeed to the soul. Notes of pure joy, wrapped in love, reverberated upward. Yes, love, years of love, and how those years had passed, 16 of them to be precise, since I had arrived on this remote northerly isle. Sixteen of them, since two darling tabby kittens had bounced into my life as the first members of my SOLI family, and 16 of them throughout which the melody of the heart has grown, threading the great mystery of Love into the tapestry of its song. Yes, indeed, threading the great mystery of the God whose name is Love deeply into my heart. As the night wore on and the hurricane at last diminished in volume, the cantata of the years rose and fell . . . and Flugga and I sang our symphony of thanks.

1

Whispering Dawn

Flugga's purr faded, my hand slipped from his shiny coat and my mind whirred, like a video machine winding a tape in reverse. It flashed wildly through contorted images. Time sped backwards then, bump, I found myself diminished in size and returned to childhood. There was something in me that was bent on hearing, something that I had heard and seen and been afraid of years before, while still an infant. Now I was nine years old and I listened, riveted, with ears stretched, until suddenly I grasped the horror of the situation. Squeezing my eyes so tightly that they hurt, I lay there rigid and afraid.

Those grotesque, goblin-like creatures were groping around at the end of my bed in the darkness. They were waving their stunted arms and, worst of all, they were peering at me. I could feel them, gaping, grimacing, pointing. Cringing further under the blankets I managed to lift my head enough to call, 'Mam.' Then the fear gripped at my heart, for my mouth, suddenly strangely dry, framed the word, yet emitted no sound, no voice . . . and so – no Mam. 'They' could hear, I knew it. 'They' could hear every rustle with their wide, ugly ears. Greedily they closed in, and at any moment my numbed throat, unable to function and call for help, was going to imprison me into their clutches. Terror crept across the dampness of my brow. Somehow, I had to make her hear. 'Mam. Come . . .' No, not a whisper of sound. What had happened to my voice, where had it gone? Frantic now, I opened my mouth wider. I needed my mother: 'Mam.' There was no reply, only silence. Mute, I froze, waiting . . .

Moments hung. I waited interminably, while mopping and mowing, wraithlike over the end of the bed, the spectres slithered and waved to and fro, winding, sliding between the oppressive shadows. Leeringly, they stretched out their misshapen fingers to paralyse my mind, to suppress. They had shown themselves before, on the top of the wardrobe. Then, only a tot, I had been tucked up in bed beside Mam. It had been at my grandmother's, Mamma (Momma) Parkes's, house, and that first experience of fear had passed quickly. It had passed at the touch of my hand against Mam's sleeping body and until this moment I had not given it a single thought more. No, for my life was secure.

I clutched at the sheet; I wanted my mother, she who could instantly comfort. I wanted her, I wanted to bury my head into her bosom and feel the safety of her arms holding me tight. I wanted to be told that it was all only a dream and that Dad was here too. Dad had come home now from being a soldier, and he was fearful of nothing. Of course, Carole my sister was here, curled up beside me and fast asleep, though she was far too small to help. Steadily the walls of the room closed in, sealing off every ounce of contact with the reality that I understood as life, and they did so in the same grim way that my larynx had sealed, shuttering away everything that was solid and safe. Wrung now with perspiration I shrank deeper into the flocks of my mattress, only daring to push my head closer to Carole. I wanted Mam. I wanted Dad. Yet I could only lie, piniored, under the pumping of my heart. 'Come, Mam . . . Come, Mam . . . Come, Mam.'

Yes, there were still strange rustlings, and was that something pressing my foot? My legs felt cold. I listened. No, it

— 2 —

had gone, though wait . . . could I really hear the sound of mutterings? 'Help. Mammy, come.' Another tremor, some-where . . . by the wardrobe? No . . . Yes, it touched the bed! Yes . . . 'Mam!'

Then, like a curtain rising, there came a click, a familiar click, indeed so familiar that it caused me to catch my breath. Stiffly I listened, and then, yes! 'Mam!' Relief was trickling, oozing, flowing and now pouring through my whole being, to the tips of my toes until the floodgates opened. My mother had somehow heard me, oh joy, she was pushing the bed-room door and I could hear her, her beloved uneven limp sounding in my direction. In a second she was leaning over my sister and smiling down at me. She looked more beautiful than I had ever seen her. I laughed up at her and easing myself from under the sheet and blankets I stretched up an arm and wound it around her neck. Peace pervaded my soul as though wrapped in soft down, and, indeed, in such a way as I have only ever experienced since in contemplative prayer. Eagerly, with another motion of my arm I sought to pull her closer. I loved her. Then, a most startling thing happened, something that I shall never forget, and it occurred as though it was the most natural thing in the world. Indeed, so natural that I accepted the phenomenon without question. I accepted that my arm sank swiftly down and down and right through her body, downwards, with swiftness, and strangely, into the oblivion of yet more peace. Falling, falling away my fingers clapped on to my chest until, in safety, I slept.

'Mam,' I said, as she was winding my scarf around my neck and tucking it into my school coat, the next morning. 'Mam, did you cum to me room last night?'

'Only to tuck you both in, like your Dad and I always do, before we go to bed. You were still awake – remember?'

'Yes . . . No . . . I mean later ron, in't middlet night?'

'No, I didn't, ma duck. Why?'

She sat down and listened, her face thoughtful, while I, finishing the buttoning-up of my thick navy-blue school coat, told her what had happened. Then, with an honesty I still associate with my parents, especially my mother, she said, 'No, love, it wasn't me. Per'aps it were . . . well, maybe . . .' and bending her head she whispered, 'maybe – an angel?'

At the time of this incident, I was, as I have said, nine years old, and the elder daughter of loving working-class parents. The two world wars were over and my father, now demobbed, was working as an engineer and fitter. My mother, trying to augment the family income, took in the interlocking of knitwear at home. I can see her now sweating over her machine. I hated the parlour, for it always seemed full of bags bulging with knitwear. There would be three bags of blue cardigans and four bags of ladies' red jumpers, a bag of babies' white bonnets, and there, in the midst of them, would be Mam, anxiously trying to meet her deadline. I knew that it was terribly hard work for her and that sometimes she stayed up until all hours in order to finish what she called her 'orders'. Accordingly, that hateful parlour-cum-workroom, deprived us, for quite a period, of our regular cosy evenings together when she and Dad took it in turn to read aloud chapters of *Black Beauty* and other children's books, which we had borrowed from the library in Eastwood, our nearest town.

Yes, the parlour was the only place that I remember seeing a furrow in Mam's brow, for you see, for the most part, she and Dad were extraordinarily content and gave us such a happy start to our lives. This being so, my greatest ambition throughout childhood, and even now there is still an inkling of the 'romantic', was to grow up, get married and to be as happy as they were. Indeed, as I look back I realize that their

— 4 —

treasured 'love' was also their greatest ambition for us, their children.

We were living in the small mining village of Old Brinsley, in Nottinghamshire on the borders of Derbyshire, and shared a D. H. Lawrence dialect with our neighbours, though in part it was by then becoming less broad. Grandmother, affectionately known as Mamma Parkes, had a house not far away. One could 'tek a short cut ovva't fields, un doun't pit', as the older locals would have said, and then if 'ya walked alongt railwi line', which seemed to shunt coal trucks back and forth continuously, excepting on Sundays, you were soon there. On Sunday mornings Carole and I were usually packed off to visit our grandmother while Mam cooked the lunch. We would skip down't field path, then later trawpse back home, longing, in the summer, to stop off and make 'ousus' from the sheaves of freshly cut corn, and tempted, both summer and winter, to clamber up into the familiar and inviting row of stationary coal wagons. 'It's a not fair,' I mumbled to my sister one day, 'that wi aye ta wear us best coats on Sundays when t' trucks arn't' werkin.'

'We'll pick egg un bacun fer Mamma instead,' Carole always insisted. I remember that for a long time she was under the impression that these tiny plants flowered perpet-ually, and was extremely perplexed when unable to find them. So, invariably, with fists full of wild flowers, we would come out on to the road by the railway crossing, then wander along past the New Inn to a row of miners' cottages, only stopping when we arrived at number 16.

My mother and I had lived with Mamma and Dadda (Dodda) Parkes while my father was away in the war, so her house, backed by a field with its winding brook, had become as familiar to me as had the life of that era. The life, I mean, before such amenities as the washing machine and television, though both by this time were on the brink of bursting into the Erewash Valley; in fact, had perhaps already done so in the more affluent homes of this area, of which there were few.

I well remember the fascination of watching my grandmother doing her weekly wash. Pristine in her wrap-over pinny, with her scarf tied, turban style, around her head, she stuffed clothes into a dolly tub full of water and 'ponched' them up and down for all she was worth. Then, if I can remember rightly, she squeezed and rinsed out 'the whites' and dropped them into the boiler that was built into a triangular-shaped brick surround in a corner of what we called the 'bottom kitchen'. On these occasions the boiler always had a roaring fire in the grate below. After this we would wait awhile before the steaming bundles could be hooked out with wooden tongs and eventually mangled. What a nice name 'dolly tub' was. Mam had made all sorts of dolls for me, rag dolls mostly, when she and I had lived for a while in that same 'bottom kitchen'. There had been a sailor doll, a soldier doll, a Dutch-girl doll, and they had all had celluloid faces, that somehow, and I still find it a bit puzzling, she had managed to fix to their heads.

My mother, a cripple, whose disability was the result of childhood polio, 'got around' as well as anyone I knew. With her determination and cheerfulness, she never seemed daunted. Nevertheless, after we had moved to our own home and Dad was back from the army for good and I, by that time, had a small sister, she made one concession in the winter and this was to move Carole out of her room into my bedroom. Carole's room, the so-called 'tank room', I always coveted because it had a view over the garden. My room, slightly larger, was on the other side of the house and in it I had a three-quarter bed, which my sister shared. In this way, since there was no central heating in those days, we were warmer and, indeed, it saved on the washing and drying of sheets and on Mam having to walk up the slippery garden path in her 'irons' or callipers, as we would now call them.

Thinking back, I can see my bedroom clearly with its round-topped, metal fireplace that was only lit if Carole or I were ill. In fact, the highlight of having the bronchitis that ailed me most winters until my teens was lying in bed watching the firelight flicker around its walls when the light had been switched off. In one corner there was that forbidding wardrobe, which on these occasions was illuminated into an unusually friendly and comfortable piece of furniture. On the opposite wall there was the square window that in daylight looked out across the lane and over the fields, framing the colliery with its enormous pit wheels.

So, childhood was simple, free and idyllic, and although there was never much money around, there was always a lot of laughter and shared joys and, of course, we were surrounded by love. Hence I emerged from those years a shy young woman and a dreamer, who realized that she was not at all destined to become the 'lady farm labourer' that she had once envisaged. Instead, I won a scholarship to a school of arts and crafts, which in those days, for such as me, seemed to lead in few directions other than teaching, and to my mind this was the first thing to be avoided. So, when our homely vicar's wife asked one day if I would be interested instead in becoming a nanny to two children of our local gentry to whom she was related, I said yes. Of course, at only 15, it took much time and effort to persuade Mam and Dad to allow me to pursue this opening. However, I was determined, for the comfortable, buxom Mrs Newbury had painted the job for me in such glowing colours that my heart longed for the challenge. 'They've a Scottish castle and a whole village, and there's mountains and a beach and a farm. Then there's the London house . . . You'd be able to go to the theatre you know, and you've heard of the Underground haven't you?'

The end result was that my parents loved me enough to gift me with the freedom for which I asked, and in so doing allowed the next chapter of life to begin.

Turning over, I twisted my body so as to accommodate the cat more comfortably. Rain was still pelting the skylight and Flugga's warm bulk on the duvet was now thoroughly wedged behind my knees. Pulling the sheet around my ears to block out the noise, I snuggled into a more comfortable position, and a whole medley of pictures, people, relatives and friends floated before me. Back, back through the years, I sank . . . Yet there was also a woman, who wove in and out of my slumbers, a woman, increasingly dear, with whom I was now becoming as familiar as the night was long.

'Is it you, Mam?' I heard myself whisper . . .

As on that night of the goblins, long ago, when a mother's love and a mother's beauty had wrapped me in comfort, I was assured now of heaven's proximity and of the beloved ones of God, intermingling, merging and delighting in us, his beloved ones upon earth. Most especially I was aware of Mary, the queen of all mothers, and of her graciousness. Yes, heaven is here with us now and in every place, it always has been . . . and what bliss . . . If only the world could understand . . . could infiltrate the wonder around us . . . could infiltrate that which is the shining of Christ from the heart. If only the world could see, however faintly, through the complexities of its own blurred vision. Yet it is for us, for each of us to discover the reality of truth in our own way . . . the reality of the truth that lies within all . . . the reality, which is so accessible that a child may see and understand and show it forth . . .

2

The Isles Call

Having sunk far into the past, I pressed down the key to my memory, fast-forwarding the video machine of my mind, and flipping through scenes of my life as a nanny. There was a country house surrounded by gardens, a tennis court, shrubs, flower borders and the happy clamour of children playing. Recollections flashed past and I recalled several years that I had spent with the family who helped open up a whole new way of life for me. This was something that I would not otherwise have had an opportunity to experience from my working-class background. Scene after scene arose, evoking memories. I stayed in the family's Chelsea residence and from there discovered the theatre, the opera house and the general excitements of the London of those days. Then there were the two sumptuous summers on their estate on the peninsula of Kintyre, where I grew to adore Scotland and the Scottish people. After that I came to the point when I seriously considered a proposal of marriage from a member of the same family – here, I released the key . . .

How clear that long ago evening now seems, that night when I did not know whether to accept, with a simple 'yes', a life crammed with all that I thought that I wanted. A night when the moonlight threw dazzling slivers of light across the dark sea and streaked the castle turrets with shadow. There we had stood under the solid walls, a refuge indeed, and during those moments, forever captured in magnificence, I was gripped by a tension that trapped. Trapped to such an extent that I, the innocent, with a head full of dreams, hesitated. I wanted to be a lady, a real lady and live in this glorious place of sea and mountains for the rest of my life, yet I hesitated, unable to speak.

'Look,' the young man encouraged, 'let's be unofficially engaged, at least to start with. We don't have to have anything announced in *The Times* . . . at any rate, not yet. Meanwhile, is there anywhere that you'd like me to think about with regard to arranging a honeymoon?'

Still I delayed, standing mute, my mind and heart hovering and then in combat.

'I'm sure there's somewhere that you've always wanted to go . . . ? His voice rose. 'Somewhere abroad?'

An excitement arose in me too that thrust aside every contention. 'Well, yes, I'd love to go to Venice, but . . .'

'Then to Venice we'll go, and tomorrow I'll tell my parents about things. My father I know will be thrilled.'

During the weeks afterwards I see-sawed from doubt to elation, from excitement to the deepest gloom. It was the 'being in love' bit that worried me, for it was not at all as I had expected. I had, of course, rung my parents and told them the news at once, and as I look back their astonishment again resounds in my ears.

'Hang on a minute, luv, let me sit down,' my mother had said, and then, 'Well, ma duck, we weren't expectin this. Now ya really happy about it, aren't ya? You're sure that you want ta be engaged as much as Simon does? And ya really and honestly sure, sure that he's goin ta be the only person in the world for you, for always? Look, ya Dad'd like a little word.'

She handed the telephone to my father and he said much the same thing. Their concern touched me, yet the surprise in their response to my announcement served only to deepen my doubts.

Needless to say, as the weeks passed the situation took its course and wisdom prevailed, though I must add that it was not a little aided by my mother's quietness. She and I had had such happy dreams about Carole's and my future weddings; in fact our chatter had become a sort of game. Though now, well, she was reticent, which was something that I had not previously known in her. Also, I was aware of a lost twinkle in her eyes and of veiled laughter, though have to admit that I could never have imagined her sadness (which Dad described to me later) or her concealment of tears. Neither Carole nor I were used to seeing our parents unhappy and were certainly not allowed to do so on this occasion. To all who knew Mam, she was a person greatly loved, fulfilled and joyful, and so this quietly hidden pain with regard to my plans of an early and likely loveless marriage became her dilemma and my father's. They most definitely kept it private, even during their further questioning of me on my return to the Midlands. Was I 'absolutely certain?' I had mumbled that I was 'sure enough!' So, heartache persisted. It was their secret and perhaps would never have been divulged to me, had Mum not died.

On a melancholy October day, only a month or two after the proposal and a week or so after the road accident that savagely snatched my mother from us, I sat with my father, feeling that our roles had been reversed. Overnight he became the ravaged shadow of the man I had known, and indeed was never to know again. He talked of Mam's unease, while I briefly explained to him that the fragile plan of my being engaged had been terminated. Looking into his glazed eyes, I told him that all my longings for a certain type of life were over, or at least on hold.

'Ya Mam,' he said, 'didn't want ta spoil anything for ya. She loved ya very much, you and Carole, ya know that, but all t' same she was upset abaat things. Her tears both surprised and shook me, they did. Ya see, she somehow knew it'd be wrong for ya and well, she hoped yad wait a bit. She'd be relieved now that it's not goin ta happen. A'course, we wouldn't a stopped ya if yad a thought it wa really right. In any case, ya'll find what your heart's lookin for one day, and ya've got plenty of time, ma girl, so don't go being in too much of a hurry now.'

I always knew that my parents loved and trusted me enough to risk allowing me the freedom of making my own decisions. Therefore, leaning on this solid grounding, I had been able to make a wise decision and to see that whatever such a marriage might offer, it should not be pursued. Of course, to one who was already a romantic, and dreamt constantly of a home, husband and children, it had proffered much, especially the bonus of Scotland with its spectacular scenic beauty, which to this day still allures. However, the basic and simple reason for bringing down the curtain was that I did not love the young man in question in the same way that I knew my parents had loved each other. For me that was the criterion.

So now, 41 years later, when I pause to remember those carefree days of pipe dreams, I am thankful that the teenager who thought that she was so incredibly grown-up had a few fundamentals in place. Yes, and that tonight, as the storm rolls around our northerly isles and she stretches her ears to catch those distant echoes, she will ponder upon how God's providence played so great a part. She most certainly hears her own young voice declaring to a disappointed youth that, of course, she liked him well enough, but not enough. More than that, even were she to marry the poorest man in the world, it would, and must, be for love.

Yet I ask myself now, what did I at so tender an age know about love? The answer is – just enough to guide me through that particular stage of my journey. For love's tiny seed had been sown in me, in the same way that it is sown in all of us by the God whose name is, 'Love'. It is strange to think now, how surprised I would have been to know that one day, love was to become my life . . . The past drifted out of reach and I think that I must have drowsed. Love . . . if only we knew your import . . .

A crack of sound jolted me fully awake. After assuring myself that the window was still holding, I lay back again into my pillow.

Yes, love could sting, and for me the arrow of tragedy had struck – straight as a die. Dark and quivering it had struck, piercing the wonder of youth and the springtime of a life teetering on the brink of adulthood, and it had hurt . . . for my mother was dead.

At once, I returned home to support my father and Carole. My sister by then was 13, an adolescent and very much at a time in her life when she needed our mother. I needed our mother too, desperately, yet for everyone's sake I had suddenly to grow up.

So, whirled back into the home that I had loved, I was forced to wrestle with a life that was suddenly incongruent, for everything had changed. My mother was no longer there, my father was broken in spirit, my sister had become a stressed-out teenager and I, like the world that I now suddenly looked out upon, was also different. Yes, the whole concept of life had changed – except, that is, for that mysteriously hidden and indefinable being whom everyone called God.

To start with, I was now seeing my working-class background from a new angle, for truly I had been given the taste of a different, more cultured lifestyle. Also, I had experienced being part of a life in which someone had mistakenly addressed me as 'Miss Pat' – and what pomposity that had created.

My eyelids closed, the past faded, but my mind, still wakeful, churned around, spitting a cluster of memories to the surface and returning me to our situation a few months later. Emotionally my father was back on his feet, or as much as he would ever be. The question was, what did the future hold for me? Suddenly I was whisked to Essex, to a picturesque village where I was walking through the entrance of a large country house called Greenwoods. The house had been turned into a home for all kinds of people in need – maladjusted children, unmarried mothers and persons suffering from breakdown. It was owned and run by the Baptist Church's West Ham Central Mission, with whom I worked for a while. A wonderful couple by the name of Padre and Mrs Bodey had been appointed wardens and most of the staff were young and interdenominational.

The Bodeys were lovely people whom I could see clearly. Yes, the husband, a Baptist minister, was smiling and he was giving me a key, the key to the door of their hideaway house, Joycroft. Joycroft was a silent, peaceful place and at once, in thought, I found myself en route there. It was my day off and I was chugging through the countryside on a rickety train. A station or two down the line, the engine wheels squealed and clanked to a stop. The scene was becoming clearer . . . now I was clambering out of the carriage and on to an empty platform. There I stood, watching the train rumble away; then, turning, I pushed open the gates of a level crossing. The house, only a stone's throw from the tiny station, was easy to find and soon I reached its door. Trees shimmered, the surrounding fields sang and I had the rest of the day to myself; that is, until Padre came later, to return me to Greenwoods.

There, in the small, book-lined bungalow, I experienced for the first time what in later years I was to call a retreat. Sunlight shafted through the windows and particles of dust danced in a pool of light across the shelves. Glancing along a row of books, one title belonging to a thin, uninteresting-looking volume sprang into focus. Immediately it reminded me of a conversation I had had with our vicar at home. He had told me about his being a Franciscan Tertiary, and how he thought that I would probably find it helpful to become one too. I had filed away in a drawer all the information he had given me and actually quite forgotten about it – until now! Tugging the book from the shelf, I tucked it under my arm and, balancing a plate and mug of coffee on a tray, made my way out to a chair in the garden. Little was I to know that the dusty volume, entitled *St Francis in the World Today*, would change my life.

Only ever had I thought of St Francis as a monk in a glossy picture in a book at infants' school. Of course, everybody knew that he had had a great affinity with the birds, but on that quiet summer's day I discovered more. I found that he was just an ordinary young man, as I was an ordinary young woman, searching for something that had proved elusive. Yet – delight – he had found it! He had found exactly what I myself wanted: 'perfect joy', and he had found it by giving up everything, absolutely everything, for God's sake. Of course, this was the way that I too would go . . . my heart knew it at once. Even so, was I courageous enough to risk everything that spelt happiness – for God? Could I love him enough . . .? Yes, I knew that I could, and in the garden at Joycroft I offered my life.

Being young and idealistic and against the better judgement

of my elders, I tested this way of St Francis at once by giving up everything I could think of: my wages, all my hopes and ambitions, and even my desires for a husband, home and family. Not surprisingly, these measures triggered off a series of amazing events. It was as though a golden pathway was suddenly rolled out in front of me, winding me forward into the future. People known and unknown to me appeared along its route, at exactly the right moment and saying exactly the right things, and so it was that I stepped on to it and into a life that was companioned by Christ. Padre heavily discouraged such fervour and I carefully did not mention it to Dad, at least not until I could persuade him and everyone else who loved me to share my joy.

Simon's father, Audwin Oakes, an Anglican lay reader who after my mother's death became an important spiritual mentor to me, was quite averse to a monastic call. He had hoped that I would train for social work of some kind; yet, in the end and without at all meaning to do so, he was instrumental in leading me towards the religious life. One day he arrived at Greenwoods to pick me up and take me to the family's Chelsea home for a few days.

The Rolls glided into the forecourt of Greenwoods and after a quick cup of coffee we threw my bag on to the beautiful upholstered seat at the back of the car and sped up to London. What I did not realize was that I was about to spend a weekend so providential that one could not doubt that it was directed by God.

On the first evening I spent in London, Mr Oakes showed me a book that he had newly bought, called *Religious Communities in the Anglican Communion*. Having glanced through its pages, I passed it back to him and waited for his own assessment of it before making a comment.

Leaning forward, he shook the volume slightly and said,

'As you know I'm not too keen on this type of lifestyle; nevertheless, there's a particular women's order that does interest me.' In a quizzical fashion so familiar to those who knew him, he raised a bushy eyebrow. 'Now, you won't go getting ideas in this direction yourself, will you? I'm only sharing it with you because I'm fascinated.' He flicked open the book and tapped down the page with his finger. 'This is the paragraph. Listen.' He read an excerpt of information about a tiny group of women living a very simple Franciscan life of work and prayer in the heart of the Devonshire countryside.

'Franciscan!' I blurted, but stopped, not daring to mention my own Franciscan leanings. Later, I asked if I might borrow the book. That night when I went to bed I spread it open across the bedspread and, kneeling down, leant over its pages. Something in me knew, and I can still feel the certainty of that knowledge, that this was where God was leading.

The next day, over breakfast, Mr Oakes asked if I would like to accompany him on a business trip to Cambridge. Staggered that such an opportunity should present itself I at once agreed, especially since for a week or two I had been hoping to visit that very location. However, on account of my Joycroft experience, I had of course been unable to do so, having had no funds! My main reason for going there was that I had become greatly interested in working with unmarried mothers and wanted to discuss options with the matron of a home for single mums in Cambridge. It should be borne in mind that this scenario was several decades ago, when such people were thought of as 'naughty girls', in need of a specialized type of care. I had discovered the home through a friend who had influenced me during my time in Nottinghamshire after my mother's death. She had done part of her own moral welfare work training at this place of caring.

Audwin Oakes dropped me off there, and instantly I wished that I could have been spirited elsewhere. Everyone was busy, everything seemed in motion and Matron had neither the time nor, I think, the inclination to see me, though 'she just might' if I waited long enough. The waiting time lengthened and I had heaps of opportunity to think about my experience of the night before. 'Why on earth have I come,' I chewed . . . Heaven only knew, and anyway there was no polite way of getting out of seeing her now. At this alarming stage I felt like a fly in a web. Eventually I was asked to 'Come along this way please', and with a thousand butterflies flapping inside my tummy, I was hustled into Matron's room.

The interview was difficult, to say the least, and not at all helped by my saying that I didn't know why I had come! Then, sipping a cup of tea without at all tasting it, I found myself blushing into the cup. Covered with confusion, I realized that she, Matron, was assuming that I was an unmarried mother myself . . . Of course, my embarrassment did wonders in opening the floodgates, and suddenly I found myself telling her all.

Mary Stubbs's face crinkled into a smile. 'You mean that you think you've got a religious vocation?' she asked.

'Yes, I'm almost certain I have,' I heard myself admitting for the very first time.

'Well, my dear, I'll tell you something now you've told me that – I too tried my vocation once, in a little Franciscan community in Devon.'

It was, of course, the same Franciscan community that I had been poring over the night before!

'Would you like me to write to the Reverend Mother?' she asked, and I said that I would.

Within a few months I had joined the Anglican Franciscan Sisters in Devon. Here, first as a novice and then as a young

Sister, Sister Agnes of Our Lady of Joy, I learnt the skills of husbandry, the tilling of the soil, the caring for pigs and poultry and, most important of all, the daily learning of God. Certainly I was educated in the giving of my life totally to God; yet somehow there was always something missing.

The night before I made my Life Vows, the Reverend Mother took me by surprise by enquiring what gift I had asked of my heavenly bridegroom. I had smiled, far too shy to tell her anything of that nature, and on that occasion she did not press.

Pressing the key into memory's fast-forward mode again, I skimmed through the first 15 years of my life with the Sisters. In some ways it was idyllic, living in that old thatched farmhouse nestled among the hills and red fields of Devon . . . though suddenly I heard the sound of the sea. My heart lurched, for after an eternity I was back in the beloved north and this time cast upon Iona, a tiny island off the west coast of Scotland. Here, strangely, I was flooded by a great sense of 'home'. Rosemary, an associate member of the community to which I belonged, had obtained permission to take me to this glorious place, where we shared what turned out to be an incredible holiday. While there, a call to bring the religious life back to the Scottish islands came to me, and my answer had been yes, yes, yes! However, the timing of God is not as our timing, and a period of seven years, undoubtedly the unhappiest and yet most formative of my life, was to elapse before the same call was repeated, this time during a visit to the island of Fetlar in Shetland.

Seven years to the day of landing on Iona, I arrived on Fetlar, having at this time been offered a second holiday to the Scottish islands. While staying on this austere northerly isle, the same call that I had had from God on Iona, that had so held me in thrall over the years, came again and in the

same, identical way. As I lay in bed one night listening to the silence around the cottage, God asked me, for a third time in my life, to let go of everything and to follow him, to do what he asked, whatever the cost. Yet on this occasion he added, in his irrevocable way, 'You can answer yes, or you can answer no, but if no, well, all right, but this is the end of your vocation as it is meant to be.' By the morning I had managed to pluck up enough courage to answer 'yes'. Yes, to all the joys that were to come, as well as to the difficulties and even to the pain that the future might hold.

Six months later, with a minimal amount of baggage and having been released from all obligation to my community, though not from my religious vows, the then Bishop of Exeter gave me the enormous privilege of testing a 'call within a call'. Thus I arrived on Fetlar with Rosemary and a handful of second-hand bits and pieces of furniture that she, by then a firm friend, had helped me collect. Since my last call had come from Fetlar this, I decided, was where I was meant to begin. Decisions were made and an amazing string of miracles happened, as indeed they continue to happen, and as they are wont to happen when one follows the ways of God with nothing to lose. The first was that I was able to rent a tiny croft-house for next to nothing and later, with Rosemary's help, to settle into it with joy. Now the time had come to live by that faith I had tested those 21 years before.

Flugga moved, then I felt him pad over me in the darkness. Slithering down the blanket he clomped to the floor. Thinking that I had better take advantage of his absence, having not previously liked to disturb the old cat's slumbers, I fumbled for a torch and stiffly followed him on to the landing. The house rocked, and at the top of the stairs I paused, catching Flugga's gaunt frame in a ray of torchlight. He was gulping down the saucer of milk I had left out for him earlier. Tiptoeing into the bathroom I lodged the torch on a ledge above the washbasin so that it spilled out a funnel of light, spotlighting the opposite wall. How silly I was, for there was no likelihood on so tumultuous a night that a creaking floor would disturb Sybil, whose bedroom was below. Anyway she, too, would be lying awake, parrying the storm. A moment or two later I eased the bathroom door shut and silently clicked the catch into place. After nearly four decades of being a religious, quietness, especially of movement, had become a part of me.

Moments later I returned to my room and, standing well back from the skylight, in case it swung inwards, I spun my torch around its frame, praying that it would hold. Better not risk fiddling around, I decided, for the slightest touch might fling my night into even greater chaos. Climbing into bed, I wondered if Flugga had trailed back behind me . . . there was neither sight nor sound of him. When he does return, I brooded, I would need to help him back on to the bed. Assuming that Flugga had traipsed downstairs to find food, I finally and thankfully plumped up my pillow and dropping my head into its depths tried to relax.

Long ago, on that other tiny isle, Iona, I had lain awake listening, but that night, in contrast, had been gentle, with only the nuances of a flowing tide to accompany the inner callings, the urgings forward of God. Before I left its shores I had heard myself promising, astonishingly out of the blue, that if this 'thing', this incredible thing that Christ asked of me, came to pass and I was convinced that it would, I would dedicate it to his mother. Yes, I would dedicate it to that woman whom I now know as the dearest of mothers, that woman whose very silence is love and who, whatever the turmoil or mistakes of our life, is to us the kindness of healing balm.

With a mighty effort Flugga scrabbled up the bedclothes, scrambling back to his favourite niche behind my legs. Slowly he twirled around until eventually he flopped into place. I leaned over in the darkness, moulding a hand around his now bony spine. 'Sorry, Flug,' I whispered, 'I should have heard you come.' What love and companionship he and Skerry had brought, especially during my solitary years here on Fetlar. Now Skerry had gone onwards and Flugga, a weary old puss, was still purring at the slightest pretext. 'You're a great example to us, Flugga,' I told him. 'Alas, one day and all too soon, you also will leave us for a while.' Yes, love hurts, at least in this world, but all will be well . . . for nothing matters but love . . . love. A voice spoke into the depths of my heart . . .

'I and my beloved Son are ever with you.'

3

The Heavens Shake

Stretching out a hand I could have touched the stillness. The stillness of a world that seemed to be holding its breath on that morning, after the night when Rosemary's caravan, her cosy, summer 'bolt-hole-cum-poustinia'[1] had been destroyed, had been blasted into a battered heap. Sister Mary Clare and I stared unbelievingly at its once sturdy frame, now chewed and mangled. What an indescribable mess; yet, out of the mess came one tiny blessing, the blessing that Rosemary herself was at that moment unable to see the shambles and the utter confusion that surrounded her home.

By this winter of the first 'hurricane', I had lived on the small island of Fetlar for seven years. The first four and a half of these I was alone, except for my Posbury friend Rosemary, a retired schoolteacher, coming and going between her home in Devon and my home here by the sea. 'Goodness, you're just like a tirrick,' the locals had told her, comparing her to the migratory arctic terns. She had heartily agreed, hinting at the same time that that was how she liked it – until she herself, suddenly wearying of flight, alighted permanently on this island of birds.

In a ridiculous way, which Rosemary never fully understood, only a fortnight after our arrival here she had found herself negotiating to buy Lower Ness, the only other croft-house besides mine on the Aithness headland. It was her first visit to Shetland, 'and I've merely come to help you to move into The Ness,' she had stressed. I must add, however, that we both found the rapidity of the negotiations and transaction to buy Lower Ness amusing as well as delightful. We often laughed that she had initially, and long before telling me, thought that I was 'off my head to settle in such an end-of-the-world place', and, she had glared, 'I've only trailed up to Fetlar because I'm determined to see you settled.' Although she made no mention of it, I knew, of course, that another factor was that she loved home-making. Also, and importantly, she was a great naturalist, not only interested in birds but exceedingly knowledgeable about them. So her impulse to buy a dilapidated property, on a bird-thronged island, next door to me, was not, when you thought about it, at all surprising. The hope that God might have marked her out as a possible fellow-traveller, vocation-wise, had also crossed my mind, though I had said nothing. So what a thrill it was when it seemed so right for her, and even more that she was in time to save a property so full of character from falling into ruin.

To start with it was not Rosemary's plan to actually live in Lower Ness permanently, for she was very attached to her home in Ilfracombe. However, over her three or four years of becoming acquainted with Shetland she had had the croft-house solidly renovated, grown to love it and was now planning to stop being a 'tirrick' and so make it her permanent home. For me, having my friend finally settled as my neighbour brought with it a feeling of strangeness. I had lived a hermit lifestyle in The Ness with contentment, yet interestingly the adjustment to suddenly sharing a part of my life again occurred both naturally and easily. The easiness I attributed firstly to the fact that I had become accustomed to Rosemary's visits over the years. Secondly, I found the sharing of the Divine Office and the rhythmic framework of

— 24 —

my life with so spiritual a friend a joy. So we lived companionably, bound in spirit by the God we worshipped in the little oratory-chapel that I had created out of one of the loft rooms of The Ness when I had first arrived. Together, we enjoyed the simplicity of our two croft-house cottages, which sat adjacent but a comfortable distance from each other on this bare sky-laden peninsula that was fringed in summer, though devoured in winter, by the great North Sea.

So it was that my idyllic years as a solitary ended with the coming of others to join me. After Rosemary's permanent arrival came Mary, a delightful middle-aged widow who, like Rosemary, was also a teacher. Mary, the first person to be clothed as a SOLI sister, was given the name Mary Clare, and shared The Ness with me, although because of the smallness of the croft-house this was something of a squash! Then came a third teacher, Frances, who was also a professional church musician. Wonderfully, she gifted us with her musical abilities, took us in hand and corrected our appalling plainsong. She took up temporary residence in one of a small cluster of island council houses; like Rosemary, with the preference of living as a friend, alongside, rather than as one who wished to become a Sister.

I thought it strange yet complimentary that SOLI should so attract teachers, especially since I had received only the most basic schooling myself. Yet the four of us somehow grew together and were united in the living out of a spiritual life within the rhythmic seasons of this wild isle. We grew in understanding and in friendship, bound within the framework and the seasons of the Church's year as well as by Mother Nature's own tides of time. We were caught up in the ebb and flow of the Divine Office in the tiny oratory-chapel and united, too, in the daily tasks which however mundane were a joyful part of our prayer and of our giving glory to God. We were bound also in our recreation and in our laughter.

On this day after the first hurricane, Sister Mary Clare and I were not laughing, however. We were, rather, a study of concentrated effort, when (and could it have been telepathy?) we each stopped and glanced up at the skylight behind which Rosemary was lying comatose in bed. We were uneasy, for she had been smitten with the current flu virus rampaging around the isle, and it had developed into one of her annual battles with bronchitis. On this occasion she could not think about, even less bother with such trivialities as storms. We darted each other a meaningful look, though said nothing. The air was thick with an almost eerie silence, left by that knave, that detestable hurricane, who having wreaked his havoc had finally whirled from our shores leaving us all, apart from Rosemary, inwardly reeling.

'This is monstrous,' I muttered after a while, 'though goodness knows we're fortunate compared to some.'

Again, we bent to our task and worked steadily on. It was heart-rending, especially seeing such things as a Bible tossed with apparent abandon into the ditch, a tablecloth torn around a fence and Rosemary's beautiful blue teapot crushed beneath a metal bar. We worked the whole morning, collecting up rubbish and carrying what was retrievable to the barn. Yet, despite all our efforts, we salvaged little of what had been our friend's pride and joy. So it was with despondency that we went off to lunch that day, for a vast portion of the ground around her house was still a devastation of soggy blankets, splintered wood and fragments of broken crockery. Even the fridge, battered and lying face down in a corner of the garden, had spooned up a handful of books and some cutlery before finally slamming itself shut.

The chaos was the same throughout Shetland, and across

our isle all that had not been anchored like iron to the earth had been swept over the waters or caught up and twisted into tangled debris. Of course, there are few caravans up here in the far north, and later, as we drove across our northern islands to the mainland of Shetland, we could see why: those there were, however strongly roped down, were wrecked. It was now evident to everyone that such temporary homes were not designed for these shores. Later on that strange New Year's Day, more news filtered through to us of horrendous damage, and even of the deaths of a couple of sweethearts, one of whom had been thrown from a cliff. Mostly, however, it was the caravans that had gone, that were blitzed and laid waste, particularly a small gaggle of them on the edge of our mainland town. Yes, again the storm-fiend had triumphed, snatching away home, hearth, comfort and security from a whole community of people.

My room continued to be bombarded, and in the blackness one could only imagine what each crash meant. Sometimes, I thought, life is like that, full of moments when one waits trustingly for God to cast his light and peace over the turmoil and to transform. Darkness, death, fear, pain, tears . . . all, in different ways, are a part of our spiritual growth, which needs enormous patience. Patience, too, is all part of the course that leads us to the knowledge that in the end all will be well. The wonderful thing is that we belong to Love, and however tried and tested we are, we know that he has a purpose for us within his incredible plan. So why is it so difficult to rejoice, when ultimately nothing can harm us unless we allow it to do so and when always, as morning comes and our darkest nights slip over the horizon, he is there? Yes, our Lord is there, continuing to lead us forward, onward . . . showing us the order of the day and, finally, into our glorious inheritance of the children of light.

Normally I love this gabled alcove where I sleep. It is a place of thinking, of retreat – of solace and of being with God. And it is most especially dear on moonlit nights when I can lie and watch the stars through its leaning window. Tonight was different, for it was a target crouched under the fury and fire of a monster. Tonight my refuge was no refuge, for it was being assaulted by the vast, fearful firmament, the great vault of heaven, sometimes veiled, sometimes challenging, always spitting out question marks. I twisted over to face the wall, restless now, and remembering the first time I was old enough to look into the skies and doubt.

It had happened on a crisp Nottinghamshire winter's night, after we as a family had been visiting friends of my parents. It was an unusual treat for Carole and me to be out after dark, yet that night was not at all exhilarating. Instead it was somehow cold and heavy. Mam was tucking Carole into her scarf, I remember, and I was asking Dad questions about the sky and wishing that the bus would soon trundle into the village so that we could get home. Staring up at the spangled myriad of stars, my father pointed, explaining . . . and life was suddenly changed and uncertain.

— 28 —

'But Dad, what about God and heaven, where are they?' Soon Mam was joining in the conversation too, and I believe they would have dealt with the question more sensitively had they but known how serious a turning point in my growth this was. Alas, I was unable to share my grappling fears and they had no idea that my childhood had rolled away that night, leaving me with a hard world of facts.

If stars are matter, I thought, then it was just space between the ground upon which I stood and the rest of the universe. All this dark sky that I could see, and there was so much of it, went on and on. The world was matter, everything was matter, so what about angels, and what was heaven and who was God? Perhaps there wasn't a God after all and the Bible was only a story. For the first time in my life I reasoned, and it seemed suddenly clear: all that could not be explained, like God, was no longer real. The child in me had known the spiritual, for the child had known love and in love had known God. Now the door of the mind had swung open to reason and was squeezing out the intuitive wisdom of the innocent. Things from then onwards would need to be proved, for nothing about God was sure any more and it seemed as though we only lived and died . . . My colourful world of childhood suddenly swung its pendulum to black and white. Life's growing pains had begun and they had to be borne, at least until my heart's understanding found its balance of truth.

Flugga twisted unsteadily into a different position and I too eased around. Then out of the darkness came the gentle reassurance of a mother's voice:

'My love and compassion are forever with you.'

4

Thunderclouds Roll

So sure was I of my vision when I arrived on Fetlar that I expected everything to happen at once. However, apart from Rosemary's coming to live next door, God sent no one to join me for the first four and a half years – that is, no one who felt called to make a lasting commitment in the sense of vocation. Yet, slowly, I came to realize that those years were vital, for they gave me the opportunity to live an eremitical life, which in itself opened up dimensions that otherwise I would never have known. Indeed, this happened to the extent that I found myself hoping that I had, in fact, got the whole thing wrong and was meant to go on and develop the solitary calling. But as we know, God possesses a great sense of humour, and it was at this point that he sent others. So for the first few years I lived as a solitary on Fetlar with virtually no money. Later, however, as we grew as a spiritual family, with the need to extend our accommodation both for ourselves and for the increasing number of people who asked to visit us, we found that our prayers were answered and our needs supplied.

The first major thing to happen was that a piece of land was given to us for the price of only one pound. This amazing gift, from our crofter friends Sheila and Andrew Hughson, was a bolt from the blue, and tossed a chunk of Fetlar's boulder-strewn coast at our feet.

'I'm no Christian,' Andrew had said, pointing towards the

place where, from the moment I had arrived on Fetlar, I had dreamt of living. We were leaning on the boundary wall around The Ness garden staring down towards the craggy outcrop of the headland. Andrew stood, stretched himself to his full height and waved his hand, 'You see if you build over there . . . that bit by the knowe . . . you'd certainly be building on rock.'

I had not the slightest doubt that we would build on rock, and indeed on those beloved rocks, though I did wonder from time to time with what we would build, for, as ever, we had no more than a pittance to live on. During that period Sister Mary Clare and I had virtually nothing in the bank and if our savings were ever above £100 we fancied ourselves rich. Of course, on my own it had been easy enough to live by faith, but with growing responsibilities it became a burden. Living on a financial razor-edge, always having to labour over whether there would be enough money to pay the next bill, became increasingly hard. As a solitary I had thought little about finance, yet when others began to join me, duties accrued and weighed more and more heavily.

Nevertheless, there was no denying that deep down I knew that to worry was to waste time as well as energy. Indeed, when I had first ventured to Fetlar I had asked God only for what was needed and no more, and that he had always provided. At first I had been supplied with a cottage and later the land on which to build; then a grant had been given to us to build Tigh Sith, in which to accommodate our visitors; and finally, and just as miraculously, we would build our home of Lark's Hame on the headland.

Rapidly, others interested in 'vocation' or needing a holiday wrote or came to visit. Often they stayed awhile and sometimes found new meaning to their lives or a different route to take on their own personal pilgrimage. A few of them became

*The back of The Ness with Jean's house (left)
and Lark's Hame (right)*

an extended part of our SOLI family as Caim members, or lay associates.[1] During the winter of that first hurricane, with only Tigh Sith at this point erected, we were discussing vocational possibilities with Pat. Pat was yet another school-teacher who had come to visit us from New Zealand, and we were now, at this point, looking forward to her arrival in the autumn.

Rosemary's bronchitis had cleared up, visitors came and went, mail continued to increase and plans to build Lark's Hame gathered momentum; suddenly the summer had come!

Yes, the blessed summer wrapped us in its warm embrace and with such cherishing that one day I was able to be out of doors without a coat. The air caressed the whole landscape and its gentle fingers stroked my skin. How welcome it was; yet the morning had an unfathomable coldness about it too, for the sun, welcome though it was, somehow could not reach beyond the surface, and my heart was chilled.

A green haze covered the elders, which leant untidily against the old dyke wall surrounding a rectangle of fast fading bluebells and the patch of grass that we called a lawn. I was reflecting on contrasts, upon how on this mild familiar morning the pattern of my vocation here on Fetlar was changing, heading into a state of ferment from which I shrank. Goodness, it seemed as though life, in an odd way, was suddenly racing out of control. It was as if existence, strapped to a skateboard, was bowling along a road on this blue, island day at a rate that gripped me with apprehension. Was some greater force, other than my own will, thrusting me forward in this vigorous fashion? Sighing, I leant more heavily on the dry-stone dyke and continued to meditate upon how my call to this far northerly isle was changing, how, whoosh, in a flash, it was compelling me, no, challenging me to somersault on to my head. With glazed and unseeing eyes I gazed into the distance of bare hills, sea and sky, knowing, despite the sudden chill, that whatever appeared on the horizon, God's route, however rough it might become, could only ever be the route I would follow.

A crackle of twigs splintered my thoughts, causing me to glance down at the fuchsia bushes that years before I had somehow managed to cultivate in the shelter of the dyke. I spotted two large eyes peering out at me from beneath the leaves. They disappeared back under an arc of branches, though left a dark bushy tail belonging to the same anatomy – Skerry's – still comically exposed. 'Has he got a rabbit?' I wondered with a peculiar mix of pride and pity.

It was at that moment, out there in the garden, that I also realized, with just as peculiar a concoction of emotions, that all the sweetness that they – my dear little animal friends, the

— 33 —

island and the pure simplicity of my life in this place – had given me had tarnished. It had somehow lost its sharpness, its lustre, and had become dulled, bleached, wan. Of course, I knew without question that I still loved every element of my life enormously, and always would, yet that love affair, that utter gladness and that deep yearning of love, was misted, lost. Or was it perhaps, just for a season, laid aside?

The feeling was heavy, as bereavement is heavy. Something was lacking. During the first four and a half years my heart had continuously wondered at its overflow of happiness, a happiness that made each day seem more perfect than the last and upon which I had awoken exultant and thankful for every measure of what God had given. Incredulous, too, that such happiness could go on so interminably. Yet now it was all suddenly different, changed, for that deep-seated delight had dried up. I was left fractious and encumbered with things, people, work, responsibilities, questions and, worst of all, decisions. Was this to be the burden of God's call to me in the future? If so, I felt exhausted before the job had ever begun and brooded, even at this moment, that I ought indeed to be getting on, that I should be 'doing, doing', with little time now to spiral inwards into my heart's 'being'. Yet, all that we do on the outer periphery of life spins out of who we are, out of whom God has made us at our centre . . . How could I return to my centre? How could the rat race have reached me here? How could I have become so caught up into being accelerated along a road that I had no wish to take, a road that seemed increasingly paved with busyness and crowded with 'musts'. Why? Oh, how much easier it would have been to remain on my own, solitary, blissfully alone . . . with only God and the cats . . .

Sister Mary Clare peered out of the croft-house door. 'Have you made out the shopping list, and did you say that there are some letters to post? I must go now, I'm afraid, before the shop closes. It's all right if I get some extra stamps, isn't it, and we definitely need milk? Oh yes, could you light the oven and put the potatoes on . . . in about quarter of an hour? Thank you.'

I smiled. 'You won't be too long, will you? Remember we've got visitors arriving off the next ferry.' Sister Mary Clare, whom I dearly loved, was a tower of strength to me despite the fact that her energy kept me constantly revolving around the circumference of our life. Nevertheless, her vigour was of the type vital to our life during those years.

Moments later, Sister rumbled off in our old car and I crouched down to stroke the small cat. Immediately, another engine vibrated into sound, this time from an enormous interior purr-box that only Skerry possessed. I lifted him on to the wall and he moved in front of me, arching his back under my chin before swiftly pirouetting around to stretch upwards and then to push his dark head into my face. He was intimating, of course, and without doubt or nonsense, that no, there wasn't a rabbit and that food was required now, yes, instantly. 'Just a few moments more,' I murmured, drawing his body towards me and brushing my face across his thick fur. Disdainfully, he flicked his large 'lugs', as our crofter friend Kenny called them. As a kitten, Rosemary had rudely called him 'Bat Ears', though now, in part, he had grown into them, his beautiful ears. I stroked a hand along the black shiny marking that ran down his spine; he liked that and his lungs burst with a renewed ignition of sound.

So as this first legion of 'musts' came marching over the horizon, musts that I had expected and even welcomed at first, I knew that God would continue to work his will in us. I also knew that eventually, after he, our Father, had sent others to join me, our life would of necessity become busier.

— 35 —

After all, 'others' had been part of my vision for this place and they would undoubtedly change as well as challenge the lifestyle that I had established for myself on this tiny island. Yet, the building up of a family in God, of a religious community, the watching over its growth, the coping with its problems and the nurturing of its happiness, I would try to accept willingly; and indeed, those things are good. My awareness of such goodness was absolute, especially since each person who had joined me so far had added her own unique quality to the life. So, wistful though I was for my past solitary years, I knew beyond doubt that there was an intricate, heavenly plan opening out far into the future, a plan to which my heart had already said 'yes'. More, I knew that the beloved designer of that plan, him to whom I had given and would continue to give every part of myself, would also continue to mould SOLI; placing it between extremes perhaps, though only in order to give true balance. Yes, he would continue to mould each one whom he had sent and according to his purpose. For he, the beloved one to whom we had all said a joyful and ongoing 'yes', was in control, and I knew that in the end, whatever the strains and stresses of our life and the tensions that we would bear, all would be well.

It was of course the 'now' that was the problem, as it always is; it was the 'now' that allowed these increasing armies of 'musts' to appear ceaselessly over the skyline, carrying with them yet heavier pressures of combat. It was the 'now' that allowed those great armies to advance. And not only to advance but also to imprison, by the very reason of our being, at last, so grandly official, of our now being the Society of Our Lady of the Isles – in short, SOLI – a recognized religious community and registered charity. Indeed we were now firmly secured to officialdom with the thick thongs of administration, the keeping of records and the paying, with both time and money, for the privilege of being important. We were now 'recognized' and 'listed', and I hated it. From this angle, yes, my heart certainly longed for the obscurity, the freedom and simplicity of the life that I had known. It longed for the life that I had lived alone in The Ness, in this dear cottage during those initial years in Shetland. 'Time' had then been an endless gift and every moment a giving glory to God. It had been an idyllic period of space when I could open the croft-house door and breathe in the salt air, when I could stand and listen to the sound of the curlew and whimbrel calling across field and moorland. Yes, it had been a time when I could catch the loveliness of mists rolling in over the distant hills and glimpse the sudden flash of gannet wings plunging, like arrows, into the sea.

W for whimbrel

The approaching chug of our car increased in volume until Sister Mary Clare roared around the corner and pulled up. Suddenly aware that I had neglected the tasks I had been asked to do in the kitchen, I dashed indoors. Pulling the pan of potatoes across the cooker, I lit a match quickly and bent to ignite the oven. At that moment Sister came in with the bags.

'Are the potatoes boiling yet?' she teased, peering over my shoulder . . .

The more demanding and intense one's call, the greater need there must be for God to test us to the uttermost, to rattle and to shake us around in the dark, to tug us in different directions, making us pliable and strong for our journey. Like athletes training for sport, we need to be fit and in the case of a Christian with the longing to run the race to which we are called. This requires flexibility, courage, patience and occasionally blind obedience to the will of God, who not only knows the course but who is, himself, the course.

Ever since the night of the 'stars', I was aware of the struggle between extremes, between light and darkness, good and evil, and gradually a healthy tension of balance with all its contrasts tightened within me. Yet, woven around it was the artless simplicity of God's love. In and out of the years it was thread, encouraging, reassuring, comforting, helping me to be patient and to trust to his love's leading. Yes, trusting him entirely, knowing that in life's cycles of rebirth, both joyful and painful, he, Love, is the perfect tension.

Tonight earth's battle of the outer elements was terrifying, yet all was well. And in a still small voice of calm I heard Our Lady say:

'Be born again into the world to give light and love and holiness to those who seek our way . . .'

5

The Beat of the Tide

Three well-proportioned middle-aged ladies, including myself, sat around the table in the large room of our visitors' building, Tigh Sith, having come to the end of a most companionable meal. It had been an hour full of laughter and in a sense had had about it a definite air of new beginnings. Sister Mary Clare, who had provided of her culinary best, now pushed back her chair and went across the room to make coffee.

'Yes, Jackie,' I continued, 'our jovial New Zealand friend arrives on Fetlar in the autumn to test her vocation. This was planned some time ago and we're really looking forward to her return.'

Our guest, an educated woman, nodded. I had collected her from the ferry only that morning. Now, comfortably settled and quite at home with us, she began filling me in on what she had said in her preparatory letter with regard to her own colourful life's journey.

Born an only child in Argentina of an English mother and Argentinian father, Jacqueline Meyer had led a sheltered, though in some ways surprising, childhood. 'My father, euphoric over my arrival, shortly afterwards gifted me with a Shetland pony . . . and that must be a very good omen,' she added, flashing a meaningful glance in my direction. 'However, my mother's family were not so impulsive. You see, when I was four years old my parents separated and my mother and I went to live with her mother, my granny. The grandparents on my mother's side were English and had been immigrants to Argentina at the turn of the twentieth century. I never knew my grandfather, but my grandmother was one of those typical Victorian ladies who are really more English than the English. She had a maid and was always very proper, making sure that from the age of four I was brought up correctly. You know, finger bowls on the dinner table and all that sort of thing.'

Sister Mary Clare set down the tray and we sipped our coffee with half an eye on the clock, knowing that soon we must wend our way to the byre-chapel to say Compline.

'So,' said Jackie Meyer, missing nothing, as she placed her mug delicately on the table, 'I see that besides the two of you here, there are also Rosemary and Frances. How do they fit in?'

Jackie was shorter and plumper than me and as I considered her question she turned her round, bespectacled face in my direction. I explained that they were friends living alongside.

'Yes,' Sister Mary Clare nodded, 'and there's also Sybil.'

Jackie looked surprised. 'Sybil?'

'We'll tell you about Sybil tomorrow,' I added, pushing back my chair and starting to collect the crockery together on to a tray. 'You must be very tired, and we need to wash up and go to Compline.'

The next morning Jackie joined the four of us for the Office of Terce. 'Mmm,' she murmured afterwards, 'that was nice. And I like the idea of having a goat in the back of the chapel. I owned goats when I lived in Africa.'

Jumping towards her and flipping my hand to the top of her head, I pressed it rapidly downwards, catching her by surprise as she moved through the low-slung lintel of the door into the glare of sunlight outside. 'I'm so sorry,' I apologized, 'but you see, several previous guests haven't ducked low enough!'

'Thank you,' she laughed.

A few moments later, we again sat with steaming mugs of coffee before embarking on the morning's work, though this time Rosemary and Frances were with us. 'Did you have a good night, Jackie?' Rosemary asked.

'Wonderful, thank you, I'm very glad I came.'

'Yes, we really admire people prepared to tackle a journey this far north, especially since the weather's not always that welcoming when they arrive,' I said.

'We like it, though!' Rosemary added, in her determined Yorkshire manner.

We chatted for a while until the others went off in their different directions, leaving me to listen with growing interest to Jackie's tale.

'Yes, well, to put you a bit more in the picture about me,' she said, 'I left home at 25, and went to the States where I found a job working as a bilingual secretary. I stayed there over the next 16 years and finally ended up as an accountant in charge of the contractual payroll. This gave me a high salary and, as you might guess, a lifestyle to match. Yes, it was a good job and up to a point I was happy, yet there was definitely something missing, something very important, something that I felt and still feel compelled to find.' She took a breath and smiled at Skerry and his brother Flugga, who were embarking on a favourite ploy of theirs, a sort of vendetta to stare me out, the whole purpose being to perplex me into producing an umpteenth dish of food.

'Yes, Jackie, go on,' I encouraged.

She smiled again. 'Mmm, well, since as far back as my confirmation I've been aware that God was calling me to give

— 41 —

my life to him, though I knew that there was no way I could consider a religious vocation while my mother was still alive. The very idea of my becoming a Sister would have caused her much unhappiness. You see, despite the fact that she was an exceedingly devout woman, who actually had been educated by nuns, there was a contradicting selfishness in her. However, I have to add that it was a selfishness that I understood. For by this time not only had she lost my father but my granny had also died and consequently she became incredibly possessive of me. Fortunately, she never had to suffer the misery that I know she would have felt at my becoming a Sister – of my "separating myself from normality", as she would have put it – for just before Christmas 1983 she herself died. I missed her enormously, yet in a strange way it seemed as though she had gifted me with freedom, the freedom to make a joyous offering of that self-same freedom. In no time at all, I had disposed of my property and belongings and arranged to join the Society of St Margaret in Boston.'

'Just a moment, Jackie, I hope that you don't mind, but I'd better see to these two naughty, "nobody loves us", furry things.' I got up, moved into the porch kitchen with the two tails in tow, first waving like flags and then quivering with anticipation. I spooned generous helpings of food first into a blue bowl and then into a red one, placed them on the floor and then, quickly washing my hands and drying them, returned to my guest grinning.

Jackie laughed, 'Ah, I see that they're being rather spoilt,' she said, and then, much to my delight, for I always warm to cat-lovers, 'I approve.'

I sat down. 'Do continue your story.'

'Yes,' she said. 'Well, as you'll probably have guessed by now, I'm rather naughty.' I pretended to look surprised and she went on. 'You'll understand better when I confess that days before I was due to arrive at the convent in Boston I decided I was going to really live it up. Yes, for that final week, what I saw as the end of a period of glorious independence, I would have a marvellous last fling. So I booked a room in the most expensive hotel I could find and revelled in the pleasure and pure indulgence of it. That is until the last day, which happened to be the first of January – a perfect day, don't you think, to start a new life? On that morning I hired a taxi to drive me in style to the convent. In fact I stubbed out my last cigarette before walking up the flight of steps and ringing the bell.'

'And so how come you're not sitting here in a habit now?' I asked.

'Because, well, you see, this first chapter of my religious life ended three years later when unhappily I left St Margaret's. It was a dreadful experience, the leaving I mean. Almost immediately, though, life thrust me into making arrangements to follow another, very different route to God, one that took me as a missionary to Uganda. This, although it was an invaluable experience, was again only temporary and eventually, after a time of discernment regarding my future, I flew to Britain. There, I sought advice from the Reverend Mother of another religious community, All Hallows, at Ditchingham. The lifestyle there so reminded me of St Margaret's in Boston that I immediately felt at home. I seemed to fit in so well that again, without wasting any time – probably I'm too impulsive – I asked to join them. Sadly, however, it was only to leave yet another religious house two years later.

'After this, and with some confusion, I got beyond caring. I was told to, "Just wait and see what God puts across your path", and that is exactly what I've been doing for 14 months. However, I must tell you this bit of my story because it's important. Your first book, *A Tide that Sings*, kept "winking at me" from all kinds of bookshelves. I'd go to the convent library and there it was. I'd pull it out, then quickly push it back in again, or I'd saunter into the cathedral shop and again, there it was. I began to think to myself, "that wretched book". You see, at that time, I wasn't at all interested in reading about somebody else's vocation. Anyway, after I left Ditchingham I sought advice from one of the Sisters, and what did she suggest? Precisely – that I read your book! I wasn't too amused about this because the last thing that I wanted was to be a Franciscan – you know, all that poverty . . . Of course, you'll appreciate that deep down, very deep down, for I'm not given to admitting such things, I felt that I couldn't have failed more miserably. At least that's how it seemed. Yet, as you know from my letter, I did read the book in the end and, well, here I am – still searching.'

There was something of a heavy silence while I waited to see if she wanted to divulge more. She flicked a sheepish glance at me, trying to formulate some carefully chosen words and then gave up.

'Well, I know that this is the third time . . .' She stopped, and in some exasperation fluffed her hand in the air, 'but maybe God's calling me here?'

I studied her face. 'You really do think that God might be suggesting SOLI, don't you?'

'Yes,' she said. 'Yes, I do.' Then, looking slightly embarrassed and anxious that I should not think of her as a 'submissive person', she straightened her glasses and sat as upright as her granny might have sat. Thereupon, with hands clasped, this wonderfully humorous and unique woman, who was later to become a SOLI Sister, deep in spiritual insights, looked me straight in the eye. 'I'm really a very strong character,' she stressed!

In later years she was to admit to me that when she first sailed to Fetlar, walked off the boat and saw me there to meet her with outstretched arms, she knew in some unfathomable way that she had at last come home.

Over Jackie's stay with us we had several more discussions with regard to her vocation. Later, after consultation with Sister Mary Clare, Rosemary and Frances, I was led to suggest that she might like to think towards the possibility of testing her vocation with SOLI. Taking into account her experience and training within the religious life and her 14 months of discernment time, we decided that, along with Pat, she should begin a trial period of living alongside us the following October.

A long, stormy night is often a time for thinking. It is also a time when one's thoughts can be thrust in many directions. What if the roof blows off, or there is a tidal wave? Well, life would certainly be changed if those things happened, perhaps to a point where it could be viewed from not only a different but also a clearer perspective. Changed also to a point where it could realign itself and where real values could be established. Yes, I told myself sleepily, all that we need to know as we pilgrim onwards is that God seeks to shape us in and through all the vicissitudes of our life on earth. Yet he can only shape us if we will allow him to do so, in as much as he says to us, 'Come . . . come, but it is your will, your own free will. Come, and do this thing that I ask of you and do it because you love me. Yes, do it, in the freedom of love . . . that all things might become possible.'

In my youth, a wise man who was both a religious and a priest once told me that I should not be afraid of allowing God to shape me. He recommended that I should sometimes take risks, 'and even if you do make one of those mistakes that we're all so desperately afraid of making, you can be sure that God will use it so that the end result will be better than if you had never tried. You see,' he continued, ' "all things" do indeed "work together for good".'

My grandmother was one who could not get her mind around the concept of moving forward into a life lived in God – certainly of moving forward into an afterlife, for she was afraid of dying. In her later years, when I used to stay with her on holiday, she would always bring up the subject. 'But how can ya be sa sure, our Pat?' she would ask. Now looking back I hear the presumptiousness of my reply, overlaid with the arrogance of youth and all that assurance of decades ahead.

One night, in my convent's enclosure in Devon, just after 'lights out' at quarter to eleven, I lay in my cell. Suddenly, in an inexplicable way, my grandmother's presence filled the room. So overwhelmed was I by this strange phenomenon that I got out of bed and, kneeling beside it, seemed to take her hand. For ten minutes I prayed, until this extraordinary happening had dissolved once again into normality.

The next day, while sweeping the entrance hall to the house, I heard the telephone ringing. Stopping, I listened, for I had that odd feeling of knowing that the call was for me. A Sister answered *it and beckoned me to come. We were only allowed telephone calls if the reason was of great import and as I picked up the receiver I knew it was Dad.*

'I'm sorry to have to ring you . . .'

Before he could say more, I asked him if my grandmother had died between ten forty-five and eleven o'clock the previous night. Flabbergasted, he said that that was exactly his news!

Our heavenly Father steers us all, without exception, through life and makes the most complicated routes straight and simple – that is, if we will allow him to do so. For always with our God he asks us to choose. He asks us, that his way should be our will.

Nevertheless, we are human and even Our Lady initially questioned God's calling of her to walk along a certain path. 'How can this be?' she had asked. Let us listen further and heed her next most glorious words of choosing:

'May it be as you have said . . .'

6

The Rhythm of Life

God often works in threes. Nine years after I had first landed on the island of Fetlar, we, the first two Sisters and our two very supportive friends, Rosemary and Frances, were awaiting the arrival of three other people. We were waiting not only for the two aspirants Jackie and Pat to join us that autumn to test their vocations, but also for Sybil.

Sybil, white-haired and gentle, though with great determination, was a retired health visitor. Having read my books, she had been visiting SOLI since the days when I had lived as a solitary. Now she was looking forward to settling on Fetlar permanently, for she had also been prompted to consider, albeit in her late sixties, whether she too had heard a call to join SOLI with regard to a lifelong commitment. God's answer to her had been a joyful 'yes' and she was, at this juncture, cutting adrift from a happily established life in her beautiful home on the outskirts of Reading.

During this time of discernment, Sybil shared her hopes with a friend who was incredibly supportive. Others in her congregation, however, were shattered at such a thought. 'But Sybil,' they declared, 'uprooting yourself at your age, and Shetland of all places.'

Speaking for everyone who has joined SOLI, I can say that each of us has learned that God works his will in many and varied ways, and sometimes he surprises us with the most incredible moves. Of course, we all have our expectations as to how we think our future is going to pan out. In fact, many of us have a tendency to work out not only how things will be at the end of the day, but also precisely how others are going to fit into the picture, and this can be stimulating stuff. Yet with our heavenly Father it is inevitably the most unexpected, the most unusual and the most unlikely scenario that in the end develops. I, for one, thought that I knew exactly the type of people God was going to send to join me. They would be the most perfect, deeply spiritual, female aspirants who had ever entered the religious life and all would be absolutely right for what I hoped would become SOLI. Yet even the apostles were not like that, and I believe that it was precisely because they were not perfect that Christ chose them. All of us are at some time asked to wait in the dark, or to go in what might seem a wrong direction. What a good test of patience that is, for God rarely tells us everything at once. Indeed, if a life is truly given, it is given – unconditionally.

So, in so far as SOLI has evolved, God has not sweetly chosen those whom the Church or the world might think ideally suited to live a particular lifestyle. Instead, he has prepared a basketful of challenges! The marvellous thing is that he does not take into account age, education, culture or even spirituality, or any of the things that so often stymie human beings. Instead, like the master sculptor he is, he moulds every type of material into works of art.

One early afternoon Sister Mary Clare and I were washing the dishes in the tiny porch kitchen of The Ness and discussing the coming of Jackie, Pat and Sybil. 'Where on earth are we going to accommodate them all?' she asked.

Staring out of the window in a dazed sort of way, wiping a dish, I found myself catapulted into one of Sister Mary Clare's brilliant ideas!

'I know,' she announced, 'let's build extra rooms on to the back of this house. We could extend the property out into the garden and it could have an upper floor and . . . oh, lots of possibilities. It's all so obvious, isn't it? In fact, let's ring our architect friend now, and see if he'll come over from the mainland and help us with a design'.

Something inside my head bellowed, 'Wait – patience – caution – beware – it doesn't feel right.' At the same time another little voice was saying, 'Yes, this is quite a sensible idea.' You're being possessive about the house, I chided myself, and it's because you can't bear the idea of your 'dear little house' being spoilt or messed around with.

Placing the last bowl into the cupboard I smiled at Sister. 'How's all this to be paid for then?' I challenged, realizing that I no longer sounded like the ardent believer in miracles who had first landed on Fetlar.

'Look, Sister, why don't you just go and sit down?' She wiped her hands on the kitchen towel and moved off in the direction of the but room.[1] 'I'll find you some paper and a pencil and you can sketch out some possible plans of how it could be made larger, you know, without spoiling it . . . you can easily do that. Good . . . there . . . sit down, here's several sheets. Is that enough? Now, is it okay if I give Alan a ring and see if he can manage a trip to Fetlar?'

She saw the look on my face and perched on a chair beside me. 'Please, Sister, it does make sense, doesn't it? I'm only suggesting that we ask for advice. Surely we're not losing anything by asking for that. We don't have to do anything or commit ourselves, do we?'

'No,' I murmured, 'and that's just as well, seeing as we've no money.'

Alan arrived a fortnight later. After he had spent a busy afternoon walking around The Ness with a tape measure and

Detail of the byre-chapel

consulting my half-heartedly executed drawings, we waved him off and made our way to the byre-chapel.

The byre-chapel is always an oasis of peace, and the rhythm of the Office soothed, its whole purport catching one up into the steady throb of that great pulse of prayer and praise being offered to God from every part of the world. Yes, catching one up into the beating tide and the unceasing ebb and flow of a sea of worship, catching one up into an ocean in which there is both a giving and a receiving of love. The strains of our plainsong faded, the service ended and we leaned into a cushion of silence. After a second or two Sister Mary Clare regally extinguished the last candles, bowed towards the altar and all standing, we filed to the back of our stable-church.

Rosemary leaned over the door of one of the cattle stalls and stroked Iona's golden nose. She drew her hand higher, tracing the shape of the goat's proud head. Then, rubbing her fingers back and forth between the beautifully curved horns, she looked questioningly in my direction. 'How did you get on with the architect this afternoon?'

Stooping through the outer door of the chapel, with sunlight streaking past me into the building, Rosemary shaded her eyes. We stepped back inside and I closed the door. Sister Mary Clare and I told our friend that Alan had come up with some super ideas, but financially such a renovation to The Ness was out of the question.

'But what about Sybil?' Rosemary asked. 'I was rather sold on the conversion possibilities.'

'Well, as far as Sybil's concerned, Alan thinks that we'd do far better to resort to our original plan of a mobile home. D'you remember, a whole village of them were put up in Lerwick after the hurricane? They look like darling little houses and he says they'd be much the cheapest option. Apparently one of them could be transported here easily and could then be sited anywhere we wanted it, preferably where there'd be a nice view.'

'They're supposed to be very strong, they look nice and are made especially for places like Shetland,' Sister Mary Clare added. 'We've got a brochure indoors . . . Come in and have a look at it, if you'd like to, Rosemary.'

'Hold on,' I butted in. 'If you remember, the last time Sybil was in Shetland, she and I actually went to look at one of these places and found that it wasn't a bit what she'd got in mind.'

'How much do they cost?' Rosemary queried.

'Sixteen thousand pounds per home, plus £2,000 to transport one to a location such as this, plus another £4,000 to make a proper cement pad for it to sit on, plus, plus, plus . . .' Quickly adding up these figures in my head, a sudden exciting thought came to me. 'Just a minute,' I cried, remembering that our Fetlar crofting friends, Sheila and Andrew Hughson, had been trying to sell their wooden Scandinavian-type kit-house that stood on one of the loveliest, though most windblown, locations on the isle, 'what about Weatherhead?' They were asking only a little more than the cost of a mobile home. 'Gosh, yes, what about Weatherhead?' I cried again. 'Why didn't we think of that before? It's got plenty of space and several people could live there. Certainly it's a possibility for Sybil, and if it were divided, well, maybe Frances too, that is if the idea appeals to them.'

'Andrew and Sheila are up at Weatherhead at the moment clipping sheep,' Sister Mary Clare exclaimed. 'Let's jump in the car and go up there right away. Would renting be an option, do you think? Goodness, if it were then we'd immediately have got somewhere to put Jackie and Pat. Come on, let's go!'

Andrew and Sheila were as enthusiastic as we were, and confirmed that they had already moved out of Weatherhead into their new home on the Shetland Mainland. They were delighted with the thought of our renting the property and even more with our hope of buying it one day.

We had a good look around and everything about the house felt right. I do not know when I have felt so excited, and as soon as I got back to The Ness I rang Sybil to share the news. Frustratingly, there was no reply and we had to postpone our delight until the next day.

'Sybil, how would you like to live at Weatherhead?' I said when eventually I heard her voice down the receiver.

'Gracious, I'd love to live there, Sister. Are Andrew and Sheila wanting to sell?'

'Yes, but they've agreed to rent the house to us, at least to start with. I think there's a great possibility that Frances might be interested too. She was away in Lerwick, yesterday, so we haven't shared this with her yet. I'll be having a word with her later today.'

There was a pause at the other end of the line and then, 'How much are they asking for it?' Sybil asked. I announced Andrew and Sheila's price and was knocked backwards by her response.

'Is that all?' she said. 'You know, I've passed Weatherhead often when I've been walking on Fetlar, and strangely – and you won't believe this – I've often thought how lovely it would be to live there.' There was a pause and then, 'Would you like it?' she enquired softly.

'Look, Sybil,' I said, 'go and make yourself a nice cup of coffee and eat the deadliest chocolate biscuit you can find. Just enjoy the thought of it all . . . at least, for the moment'.

'I'll do that, and I'll think of which of my friends I could ring . . . to ask advice, I mean.' My heart lurched: Sybil really did feel drawn to the idea. 'Sister Mary Clare,' I called, 'D'you want to say a quick hello to Sybil?'

Later that same day Sybil rang back to tell us that she had been in touch with her bank manager and that, staggeringly, and she could hardly believe it, she had exactly that amount of money in a 90-day release account. 'Are you sitting down and listening carefully?' she asked. 'Then please understand that I want you to go ahead with arrangements to buy the property. I would like to buy it for SOLI and you can tell Andrew that I'll bring him the cheque when I come up in November. Oh yes, and did you ask Frances if she would be interested in sharing the accommodation?'

Frances was interested, and in fact moved into the house a week or so later, with the arrangement of paying rent to Andrew and Sheila until Sybil came in November, when Weatherhead would officially become ours. A month after Frances's move, Pat and Jackie arrived, full of cheer, and a short while later they joined her in the house on the hill.

I switched on the light. Amazingly it came on, despite a menacing flicker. Looking at the clock I saw that the night was half through, though there was little abatement of the storm. A flash made me snap off the lamp and quickly lie down. Almost immediately, a squealing sound pierced the darkness. Shooting up, I fumbled for the light switch again and dazzled by the sudden glare looked around to see what had happened. On the floor a bedraggled grey creature, twice the size of a normal cat, looked pathetically up at me.

'Mooskit, you're absolutely sodden! Just a minute.'

Tumbling out of bed, I pulled a wodge of tissues from a drawer and rubbed him down. He loved this, and the more vigorously I rubbed the better he liked it. Arching his back he circled around and around, pushing against my legs and demanding more. After that came the gentle head-butting routine which was another way of saying, 'Now the food!'

Flugga was curled in oblivion on the bed and was still there when I returned upstairs from ministering to Mooskit, who had followed me back complaining bitterly. Having discovered in no uncertain terms that the night was too fearful to try the cat-flap again, he was wanting to know exactly what I was going to do about things. He needed to go out, and there was no way he was going to use that emergency litter tray thing inside the back door. Switching off the light, I again lay down, conscious that Moosy was still sitting by the bed, considering his options. After a moment or two a ton weight landed on one of my arms and placed a heavy paw on my neck. Then it pushed a furry face into mine and after some communication between my fingers and its nose, I persuaded it to move in the opposite direction. Wheeling around it finally settled for the night, tightly pinning my bulk between itself and Flugga.

It's lovely the way cats wheel around, I thought, and in an interesting way it reminded me of SOLI. In fact, when the community had first begun I had used the symbol of a wheel to describe us. Now, as the years have rolled onwards, and hopefully one is wiser and less constrained, I have realized that the wheel symbol was much too wooden. Gradually the structure had begun to evolve into a spiral, a vibrant and living spiral – 'a sun spiral', within which was life and movement. SOLI was to live and emanate the warmth and love of God from its centre. SOLI was to be a type of Christ, a living symbiosis, and about this, I decided, closing my eyes again, I would write another book.

Trying unsuccessfully to turn myself around, I continued to ponder. Yes, I had been told that there is a spiral in everything and that was wonderful. For, unlike my original wheel circles, the convolutions of a spiral are not confined. Rather, as in the case of SOLI, they are living organisms made up of people with freedom of growth and movement: people who are vehicles, embodiments, channels of love, soaking up love – the love of him who at the centre, the core, the heart of life, is Love. The motion of this love within any cell or 'spiral' of SOLI is like a current perpetually ebbing and flowing, giving and receiving, pulsating and radiating out the intensity and joy of loving. Radiating out, like the stars of the Milky Way, all different and yet from a distance patterned into one gigantic, living shape.

I could not see the Milky Way at all tonight . . . in the same way, so often we cannot see the miracles of life, even less understand them. Yet somehow one knows, with a surety that emerges from the aeons of time and the depths of our own nature, that they are of the truth, the truth who is Christ. Closing my eyes, Our Lady's words again came to me:

'My Son is forever in all souls . . .'

7

Blessings of Home

Shetland for us
 Shetland for me
  Shetland for us
   Shetland for me
    Shetland for us

Lolling my head sideways, trying to keep my eyes open so as not to miss any of the landscape that flickered past the train windows, I was beginning to begrudge every moment spent away from my Shetland home. Shetland is, supposedly, a part of Scotland, though I have met few Shetland people who feel that this is so. Indeed, for those of us who live there it is a unique land in its own right, one that seems to relate as much to Scandinavia as to Scotland. Long ago I had fallen in love with Scotland, with its mountains and valleys and mystical isles. Now the sturdy, unyielding, unsophisticated simplicity of Shetland had captured my heart, for under its crusty exterior it also had a soul to be loved. In a way I have always known that the further north I travel the happier I am. On this grey morning, having ploughed 14 hours southwards across the North Sea to Aberdeen on board the *St Clair*, I was now train-bound. Speeding through a beautiful, yet in places what seemed to me, in contrast to Shetland, a stiflingly civilized Scottish east coast, I was on my way to the launch of my second book in Edinburgh.

At last, succumbing to the pull of drowsiness, I shut my eyes and allowed myself to be rocked by the train. In so doing, I swapped a misty huddle of station buildings and rows of warehouse roofs for brighter images of home.

Sister Mary Clare was driving Jackie and Pat over to the Shetland Mainland today with the intention of leaving them at Da Gaets for a month. I wondered how they would all be feeling – happy, I hoped. What would they be saying, and would our two newest recruits be enjoying the Westside landscape? Stretching out a cramped leg, and trying unsuccessfully to get my head into a better position on the much too high headrest of the train seat, I gave myself totally to the Shetland scene . . .

Yes, the car was winding its way through the Culswick valley to Da Gaets. I could see it all so clearly. Jackie and Pat, now postulants, clad in their navy-blue fishermen's smocks and trousers, with scarves tied around their heads, peered at the bare, treeless landscape. Hills rose on either side, their naked contours exposing a beauty that never failed to lift my spirits. Sloping away to their left, down a bank and beyond a rickety field fence that flanked the single-track road, lay a belt of bleached marshy ground, a lanky thread of vegetation that was dotted in winter by dark, rippled pools. The ridges of high land seemed to protect against any intrusion, clapping the vale into a timeless and rugged solitude.

Facing into the valley, immediately along the roadside, stood one, then a second, and then a third, croft-house cottage. The first was empty, the second had been renovated, with a sharply pointed roof, and the third, although inhabited by an old gentleman, had long passed its 'best before' date. The road now dropped away down a steady incline and the marsh to their left began to widen into an inlet of water.

The car continued on, coasting ever nearer to the azure

strip of sea at the mouth of the valley, of which our travellers had been getting the odd, exciting flash. Suddenly the road came to an abrupt end, wedging itself into a spur of brae that descended from their right and sloped on downwards to their left. There, it dipped the hem of its spartan garb into the cove, a Shetland voe – a kind of mini Norwegian fjord. Here, perched on a narrow plateau above it, brooding and beautiful, stood Da Gaets. Solid and strong it stood, framed by its backcloth of water and rounded hills. The loftiness of the hills drew one heavenwards and at the same time their skirts, steeped in the shimmering waters, sang out that the earth itself was but a reflection of heaven. My heart lurched, for the whole scene had a presence . . . a steely strength, seemingly culled from the beginnings of time itself.

On the first occasion I had seen the place, I distinctly remember standing at the roadside, riveted by some strangeness that thickened the air and yet at the same time remained unseen by human eyes. It was the sort of presence that dared me to cross the threshold of its mystery, its almost tangible permeation of generations of family folk who had sweated and toiled, laughed and cried. I braced myself; yes, there was pain here at Da Gaets, and that pain had to be faced. There was a hurt that somehow wrung the elements around its four walls. Its anguish was audible in the cry of the gulls and the roaring voice of the wind. Sometimes it seemed as though it had become, in itself, a sharp spear, piercing the gut. The pain of it had scraped and gouged, scooping out a cavity that now waited, longing to be filled; waited endlessly for the satiating, overflowing power of God.

In my mind's eye, I saw Sister Mary Clare pull on the handbrake and, sitting under the shadow of the hillside, gaze sideways at the house. 'How gorgeous the water is today,' she said. 'Of course,' she went on, 'it's fairly non-existent in the

Da Gaets with Barney and Pippin

summer – dried out, you know. Though in the winter, and really we only seem to have those two seasons up here, it's spewed up from the Atlantic, just over there. It's fed from the opposite, northerly direction, from a plethora of springs.'

The train chugged onwards and I delighted in the sudden seascape that spread across the window; that is, until I thought again of our own sea-surrounded isles and my family pulling their luggage from the car and slamming its rusted doors shut.

Sister Mary Clare bent, looped an extra bag around her fingers and led them down the somewhat precarious path to the house. 'Are you all right?' she called. 'Put something of what you're carrying down on to the grass if you need to. The pathway's very narrow and can be slippery. We can easily come back for things.'

'It's okay,' one of them murmured, while the other bent and disgorged a couple of bags from her hands.

'Sister Agnes loves this place,' Sister Mary Clare yelled through the wind.

There was a leaden silence, which jolted me into an awareness of Jackie's reserved manner. Regrettably, she had disengaged herself from Sister's enthusiasm. She skidded a little, stooped, held on to a tussock of grass and dropped off another bag. Then, 'Yes, it's nice,' she sighed, without sounding in the least convinced. She had, of course, already visited Da Gaets briefly, on her first trip to Shetland. In later years, when she was able to describe her feelings more freely, she said that her heart had sunk on both her first and second visits there. She had felt an ominous certainty that this place was to be a part of her destiny.

'It's rather austere,' said Sister Mary Clare, reaching the door. Realizing that she ought to sound much more encouraging, she added, 'But it's got something. Actually, Sister Agnes wrote most of her second book here and, believe it or not, says that in a one-to-one with the place, it can be inspiring . . .'

There was a squeal of wheels, and the train shuddered to a stop. Opening my eyes, I watched a swarm of people press towards its doors as they slid open. 'Auch, we'rrre here, bairns,' a lady called to her children, while another nudged her companion into reaching over my head to pull suitcases from the rack. After ten minutes of clamour, the doors slammed to and the train wound its way out of Dundee and over the Tay Bridge.

Ah, super, more water, I rejoiced, peering through a pattern of ironwork and watching gulls wheel over a flotilla of boats dotted below. Once over the bridge and a mile or two down the line, my eyelids fluttered again and I returned in longing to my beloved northern isles.

Listening to Sister's voice tapering off, I wished that the postulants could be seeing the place through my eyes. Yes, somehow it deserved credit . . . Certainly I owed it great thanks for what it had given me, for all those times I had felt a gratitude and even a love for the way it had seemed able to draw one outside the dimensions of normality. Goodness, I chided myself, how stupid can one get? Yet there was definitely 'something other' about Da Gaets – this had been obvious from the start. Rosemary had never liked it, for precisely that reason, and even I on rare occasions had felt an odd sense of fear. In the end we had had it blessed, with a bucket of holy water. Our priest friend Keith had suggested the blessing when he and his wife Eunice, who are Caim members, were staying in the house for a holiday. Afterwards the place had felt much lighter and less threatening, though still, at its heart, it held some hidden, perhaps never to be revealed, secret, some heaviness of the past.

Those few hours of daylight that I was used to experiencing in the far north in November, I was now seeing from the train as sun-blessed, though cold, not at all like the grey stuffiness of the carriage. I felt that our two new postulants would want to get into Da Gaets quickly. As already mentioned, Jackie had had a previous glimpse of the place earlier in the year, though that had been a summer visit, which was quite another matter.

Precariously, they clambered to and fro, lumping their bags of bedding, towels and food along the steep, uneven path that dropped to a square extension on the back of the house. Then, struggling further down two dangerously deep-set steps, Sister forced the swollen extension door open and they tumbled inside. I visualized them clustering around in the gloaming for a moment or two, while Sister Mary Clare located the key and opened the inner door.

'Now, only two more steps down and you've arrived,' she told them. 'There,' she added, as they gathered inside and dropped their bundles to the floor, 'isn't this nice? That's good, I'll turn on the water and the electricity. This room, as you can see, Pat, is the kitchen.'

'Oh . . . er . . . I see, it's got a zingy window,' said Pat.

'Mmm, being so large, it gives a gorgeous view of the inlet, and you can actually see a sliver of sky above the hilltops from here, too. It's about the only downstairs window where you can, unless you bend low and look upwards. The room itself, and I know it's narrow, was the original Shetland barn; a door was cut into it from the house on that side. Eventually, not all that long ago, it was converted into a kitchen. At that end a bathroom's been partitioned off, would you like to . . . ?'

'Yes, please,' said Jackie, scuttling off in that direction.

For such an old house I had always thought that the bathroom conversion was impressive. It certainly had the best view, since it possessed the only window that faced both sea and sky. However, it was also the coldest room!

Sister Mary Clare and Pat picked up some of the bags and walked through the narrow doorway that led into a larger, darker room. This was square and had an archaic Rayburn set into an alcove of the chimney wall. Two windows sat opposite to each other, letting in a little light. One looked out over the valley and the other was deeply set into the thick, exterior back wall of the dwelling. This small back window, as with all the windows on that side, faced into the hillside rising steeply behind. The road along which Sister had earlier driven was stepped up considerably higher than the house level and from this aspect one had a marvellous view of the car wheels!

'Now, I'll put the kettle on whilst you two take a look around,' Sister called brightly through the gloom, hoping to insert cheer into their disquieted spirits.

Soon they were all sitting on wooden croft-house chairs

around the table in the but room, hands clasped around steaming mugs of coffee. Hot-water bottles had been tucked into the beds to air the damp-smelling mattresses. Darkness was now dropping its canopy over the valley. It reached deft fingers into every corner, until finally it settled its dark shadows around Da Gaets.

The train squealed into Edinburgh's Waverley station and I peered through the window to see if I could locate our Edinburgh friend and Caim member, Joan McLean, with whom I was staying.

'Yes, Joan,' I said over supper a little while later, 'it sounds tough but I want Jackie and Pat to spend a few weeks at Da Gaets experiencing Shetland at its rawest. The idea is that they return home to Fetlar for Christmas. Of course, they are both familiar with life at its toughest. Jackie's worked in Africa in the missionary field and Pat's brought up five children in New Zealand. So the situation is, when Sister Mary Clare's settled them in, she's going to return home and leave them to survive a week or two together at the end of the valley.'

After the book launch, I too returned home, and we all of us battened ourselves down for the onslaught of winter.

Of course our stalwart postulants did survive, admirably, and I began to see that the experiment was saying something more to me about SOLI's specific call forward. Because of its isolation from Fetlar, Jackie had hated the thought of living out at Da Gaets, yet at the same time she knew that the challenge was essential in God's calling forth of her into the future. Though into what, that was the question, and this was what we all wondered. How could she, or we, have possibly seen, at that point, how unique a ministry would develop?

Yes, undoubtedly we 'see through a glass darkly' and are meant to do so. Certainly, for a while I could not fathom what our Lord was saying to us, except for the absolute belief that we were to take one step at a time in faith. This particular route of SOLI's may seem a strange way to proceed, especially to those who have embraced the religious life. Yet I earnestly believe that we tread the finest of lines in the following of Christ. The great thing is to discover, and to do, what he wants of us as individuals and as a community. Then, however simple or incredible that might be, and without being over-influenced by what he has called others to do in the past or what other like-minded people think we ought to be doing, we should follow our path with joy. Yes, and we should do so bearing in mind that the 'Sabbath was made for man and not man for the Sabbath'. I am now fully assured that all will be well if we go forward in the Father's way, with our hands firmly placed in Christ's. Indeed, Christ is the Way, and if we are wholly concentrated on and in him, if we are each prepared to be a tool in his hands, he, and not we, will create . . . and what wonder there will be in that.

So, it began to strike me that having Pat and Jackie at Da Gaets was right, strange though it may seem, for it had become a kind of embryo nursery garden, a place for nurturing and establishing, a place for digging-down spiritual roots. On the strength of this it was decided that they should return to Da Gaets after Christmas for a few more months, the plan being that Sister Mary Clare and I would visit them as regularly as was possible. This 'distance learning' has continued with SOLI, for now, almost a decade later, Jackie is our Novice Guardian, still living far away on the Shetland Mainland, at the same time looking after those testing their vocation. The distance itself gave to our postulants, as it has given to succeeding vocations, a greater opportunity to respond in a more mature and natural way. It also gave them an opportunity to make something out of nothing for God, primarily in the making of a home out of what they were given rather than what they thought that they ought to have. In most religious communities, especially in the past, the opportunity for a woman to make a home has been stamped out. For us, however, it is our resolve to turn such natural, domestic and warm instincts into something positive and good. Consequently, 'convent' is a word we do not use, for we do not want to live in anything that sounds so institutional. Instead, we are each asked to live in our own home-cell, to live in a 'home' that we are expected to keep clean, tidy and welcoming. And to do so remembering that our Lord Jesus Christ shares it with us. And that in it, from it and out of it, we are to show him forth.

As the winter increased in vigour and the damp patches on the loft-room ceilings spread and then dripped trickles of water into buckets, Jackie and Pat returned to Da Gaets. There they learned the daily lessons that our Lord had to teach them, including the salutary knowledge of each other's failings. In this way, their unusual testing to a life in God began. Nevertheless, I must mention that their difficult times were highlighted by joy, for in such situations and in contrast to the hardships that one has to bear, the tiniest, most humble things can be transformed by gladness and blessing. One notices a sunbeam, tossed into a dark corner where it illuminates and makes beautiful; one notices a warm flame creeping up a cold chimney . . . and one is acutely aware of the stillness and peace of the hour when the storm rests.

So the life developed; but sadly for us Pat decided not to pursue a religious vocation and returned to teaching. There was no shame in that, for we are very conscious that we, SOLI, are but a stepping-stone to the next stage of life, whether that be a deeper commitment within the community or on to whatever else God in his wisdom has prepared for the seeker.

Before Pat's departure, I arranged to have a couple of nights at Da Gaets, where I was given the usual bear-hug welcomes. From the word go, I noticed that there was an air of secrecy about the pair, something akin to excitement. Suspecting that I would soon know the reason for this, I feigned nonchalance! And I was right, for in a short time, unable to contain themselves further, they told me how they had moved the chapel from the increasingly mouldering porch to the space under the stairs. The space was, in fact, a tiny room with a window facing the hillside. I had always thought that this bit of the house was special and that whatever one did with it, the slope of the stairs rising through its ceiling would make it pleasing. Immediately my mind set about balancing the sort of furnishings that might highlight its characteristics and how best to do so with what little wood and financial resources we had.

'Come and see,' said Jackie. 'You show her, Pat . . .'

Clamping my mouth shut I suppressed my urge to make creative suggestions, for this was their project, their offering, and they were thrilled with what they had achieved. Pat had made a crocheted frontal for the altar as her parting gift, which I liked and said so, and Jackie had made two beautiful altar-cloths and had found a pair of candlesticks. 'It's nice, isn't it?' they said, and I declared that it was. Then Jackie gave me the best and most generous surprise of all. 'We thought you'd like to give us some help and advice about seating.' Within a comparatively short space of time we had eaten supper and guess what? I was wielding a hammer!

Pat was leaving us the next day, a day that dawned to a snow-laden sky. There had been heavy falls through the night and the landscape was virginal and silent. Down through the valley, freshly covered mounds lay along the roadside where a plough had already cleaved a track for the post-van.

O for oystercatcher

Stumping up the now treacherous slope to the road with Pat's suitcases and boxes we pushed them into the car. Pat had cleverly managed to get herself both a job and a house close to the school in which she was to work. This was situated in a much more civilized area of the Shetland Mainland, 40 miles or so south of Da Gaets. So, hung around with hot-water bottles, we slid away along miles of single-track road. Then, having seen her into her new abode and after a tearful farewell, we returned home.

I could hardly wait to pick up my tools and continue our work on the new chapel, for I badly wanted to complete the job before I left for Fetlar the next morning. Of course, there was now some element of doubt as to whether the weather conditions would actually permit me to leave.

'I'll cook the supper while you make a start on things,' Jackie nobly suggested, and I needed no further inviting.

Later, after we had eaten, she offered me a hand and tells me now that after that evening of frantic creativity, through a power-cut and partially in candlelight – when she swears that I almost sawed off her ear – she felt, quite suddenly, that she had got to know me!

Had I slipped into sleep? Yes, I must have done, for I had awoken abruptly out of a dream, the details of which slithered away as I was flipped back into the roar of the storm. Having eased my shoulders from under the sheet, I snappily returned to the warmth, ducking my head under the seeming safety of the duvet. Would the racket never cease?

I tried to remember the dream . . . no, it had totally gone. Despite the fact that I do not often remember my dreams, I began to ponder upon the strangeness of a whole series of them that I continue to experience to this day, always about a beautiful mansion. Smiling, I thought of what someone who understands such things might say of me! Each time, I find that I am returning to a house or castle that looks quite different from any I have seen before. Yet always I return with elation and find that inside it is the same beloved place that I know and that it is located in Scotland.

There was another whiplash of wind on the window. Realizing that I was unlikely to sleep for a while, I wondered whether to get up and make myself a drink. No, I decided lazily, I was much too snug.

'Yes, houses,' I thought . . . In my imagination I often return to the house in the Culswick valley, especially at night. The austerity of Da Gaets was an important part of SOLI's growth and in our early days of using it, it was for me a thinking place, a place that blasted away the cobwebs and braced the soul.

For Jackie, later to become a SOLI Sister, it was an essential training ground for the vocation towards which God was leading her, a vocation both contemplative and yet touching the hearts of ordinary people. It was a vocation that drew into a circle of friendship housewives she met on the bus, tourists who wandered down Da Gaets pathway to the beach and local Christians from other denominations. For Jackie, the house also became a place she could make a 'home', and this I have always encouraged SOLI to do.

As already touched upon, it seems that within the religious life there has been little concept of 'home'. For me, I think it is a vital part of what SOLI has become. 'Even the birds of the air have their nests,' and goodness knows, the holy family themselves lived together in their holy home at Nazareth. Surely, then, home should be a place of joy, a place of 'being' together, or even of 'being' alone. A place that can become an extension of who we are and whom God is asking us to be.

Since the day I arrived in Shetland to make my home in The Ness, it became just that, a cosy home in the winter and a place open to the wide, beautiful spaces of moorland, sky and birdsong in the summer. It certainly became my meeting place with God, a place of 'being' with him: a simple, glorious place, into which I could invite those who knocked on my door. And yes, it was not only an extension of myself but also a temple of God.

Jesus has told us that in his Father's house there are many mansions; the modern Bible translation says, 'There are many dwelling-places in my Father's house'.[1] In other words, there are many places of abiding in him.

'Open your heart to him, that he may be within all your lives . . .'

8

Ripples of Light

The winter snow melted and whiffs of Shetland's almost non-existent spring wafted around us in the decreasing winds. The morning was a steely one and Sister Mary Clare and I set sail from Fetlar on one of our monthly visits to Da Gaets. On board the small roll-on-roll-off ferry we swung through a heavy swell, ploughing stalwartly against shoulders of wind towards Yell. Spasmodically waves surged and broke over the prow, shooting fountains of salty water across the deck and spilling rivulets of spray down the car windscreen. During most of our northerly year, conditions are such that it is as well to stay in one's vehicle when travelling by sea – Leviathan is never quite so quiescent that he can be trusted. No, the mighty North Sea, rarely known to show deference, is apt to surprise with a contrariety of moods. Indeed, the waters around us, in their eddying, flowing, crashing and raging moods and not least in their gnawing into our vehicles while partially submerged on a crossing, are greatly to be respected.

Half an hour later, the ship's engine groaned to a stop and slowly its visor cranked upwards and jerked open. Like the widening jaws of a killer whale, it gradually revealed to us, as though we were Jonah, the ferry terminal of Gutcher. Gutcher is a hamlet consisting of a few houses and a post office. Rather wonderfully, it also provides a warm, well-equipped café – an enormously appreciated facility, especially on a winter's eve when island folk would otherwise have to suffer hours of buffeting, arctic conditions while waiting for the ferry.

One of the ferrymen squeezed past our car, opened the flap of a small box on the starboard side of the vessel and pressed a button. Rattling violently, the ramp jolted downwards and clanged into place. I switched on the car engine and waited to be waved forward. Gliding off the deck, we rolled over the ramp and on to 'the island of peat'. From here we sped the 18 miles westwards to the Sound of Yell. Half an hour later we arrived at another terminal and found that our second ferry was docked and waiting to take us, with the next conglomeration of cars and trucks, over to the mainland.

Jackie had been a postulant with us for almost six months. Having come through this first part of the process of testing her vocation, it was now time for us to make arrangements for her to be clothed as a novice. So, having arrived at Da Gaets after a 50-mile drive plus the two ferries, and having eaten the welcome lunch she had prepared for us, we sat around her low, circular table and discussed the coming ceremony from every conceivable angle. It would, of course, take place in the byre-chapel on Fetlar.

During the proceedings we paused to have a cup of coffee. While drinking mine I noticed that Jackie was looking across at me in the meaningful way that she has.

'What?' I questioned, quizzically.

Looking down at her hands, she fiddled with her fingers for a moment or two, then, batted her eyes in my direction. 'Have you . . .', she was wheedling now, 'have you chosen a name for me yet?'

'No', I said, 'we haven't.'

Her face fell, and again dropping her eyes she stared silently at her hands, now motionless on the table.

Waiting for a while, I smiled. 'No, we haven't, for the

simple reason that we're going to choose it for you in our little chapel this evening!' She sat upright, her face instantly alight. 'What I suggest,' I hurried on, 'is that we shortlist 12 of our favourite saints' names . . .'

'Such as Bega,' Sister Mary Clare laughed, 'or there's Modwenna and Maelruba or Ninian. Then there's Serf, that'd be nice wouldn't it? Or perhaps Gertrude . . .'

'Stop it,' I laughed and turned to Jackie. 'Don't listen to her. What I'm proposing to you is that we cut up 12 slips of paper and write the names we like best on to them. In other words, we'll have a sort of draw. We'll need to fold up our bits of paper tightly so that we can't see the names we've written on them. Then, Jackie, if you've got a bowl or a basket or something, during Compline we'll pick one of them out as your new name.'

Jackie chortled and looking enormously pleased produced a box of pencils and some paper right away. She and Sister at once began calling out the names they preferred, and needless to say I had my own ideas too!

'Bear in mind that whatever we choose is going to be prefixed by "Mary",' I murmured. We already had a Mary Clare and had decided that since SOLI was dedicated, as a community, to Our Lady, it would be nice to add 'Mary' to everyone's name in religion, including my own. 'So,' I said, 'let's actually include Mary on the slips.'

Jackie, who had by this time jotted down half a page of saints' names, glanced up from her scribbling. 'I was just Sister Jacqueline at All Hallows.'

'And what did you say your name was at St Margaret's?' Sister Mary Clare asked, flipping through a dictionary of saints and pressing it open at the next initial.

'Oh, I was Sister Mary Gregory when I was a novice with them.'

Smiling to myself, I wondered, just fleetingly, how permanent whatever name we chose for her this evening would be. Yet somehow, deep inside, call it instinct or what you will, I had a feeling that all would be well and that whatever happened, she would persevere.

'Most of the apostles' names are nice,' I said. 'Actually St Andrew would be appropriate, wouldn't it? Mary Andrew – lovely! Then of course there are the archangels. I love the names Gabriel, Raphael and Michael . . . really, I don't know which of those I like best . . . and what about some Celtic names?' I bit the end of my pencil. 'Unfortunately, we can't have Columba because that's Rosemary's name in religion and she says she'd rather we didn't use it until she's gone to glory. We'll have a long wait, I suspect! Anyway, there are some other lovely ones, like St Bride or Bridget, and St Aidan and St Cuthbert and . . .'

'Sister Agnes, do stop it, you did say that we could suggest a few as well.'

'But you already have.'

As it turned out, we all liked the same sort of names and joyfully shortlisted 12 from two or three dozen. Cutting the slips of paper to an equal size, we wrote on each one of them the full title of the Sister-to-be: Sister Mary Andrew, Sister Mary Cuthbert, Sister Mary John and so on. Folding our papers so that we were not able to see even the smallest squiggle of what had been written, we dropped each into a basket and placed them on to the altar.

At last Compline arrived and it was with great anticipation that we knelt in the little chapel under the stairs. We had decided to incorporate a period of silence into this beautiful office of night prayers, so that we might each pray that God's will would be done. We so wanted God to choose Jackie's name in religion, the name that she, hopefully, would carry for the rest of her life. Peace cushioned us until, reluctant to disturb the stillness, I stood and gently moved forward to indicate that Jackie should come and kneel before the altar. After a short general prayer, asking God that the right choice would be made, I lifted the basket, jostled it and with my eyes closed pulled out one of the slips and ceremoniously gave it to Jackie. Placing the basket back on the altar I turned back and looked down at Jackie. Sister Mary Clare glanced across at me and smiled.

'Go on, open it,' we clamoured.

Seconds later she was beaming at us. 'It's staggering,' she said. 'And you know it's absolutely right . . . perfect. It even fits in with my reading of the other day. Oh! I'm so pleased, thank you. It's amazing really . . .'

'What is it? Come on, tell us. Don't keep us in suspense like this,' Sister Mary Clare gasped.

'Well, what I do know is that you'll be as delighted as I am. It's . . . well, it's – Sister Mary Aidan.'

We stood, entranced. Yes, she was right, the name could not have fitted her more perfectly, she was – Mary Aidan.

'Come here, let's hug you,' I cried.

Half an hour later, Compline over and night drinks in our hands, a glowing Jackie whispered goodnight and without further ado went off to bed – wanting, we knew, to read more about Aidan!

A few days later, back on Fetlar, I walked down the right of way to Tigh Sith. It was a peaceful evening and the sea, a mantle of silver blue, lay cast about our peninsula. It flickered incessantly like myriad gems, except where limpid pools of glassy stillness seemed poured at random across its expanse. One day, in the not too distant future, our new home would stand on these 'banks', encompassed by this panorama of loveliness. Visualizing the building's wooden walls, its levels of roofing, its single chimney and its fascinating yet simple architecture, I stopped, held by the silence. For so long this house had seemed no more than a flimsy dream, yet now in my mind's eye it was rising out of these very rocks and rapidly growing into one of those miraculous realities of God.

Bishop Bruce had helped start off the process by suggesting that we have a 'day' that we set aside as a focal point. 'A day,' he said, 'that we can tell all your friends about, a day that we can share with them, a day when we can bless the site and, hopefully, get the building project for Lark's Hame started.' Both Bishop Bruce and Bishop Fred, the retired bishop emeritus of Aberdeen and Orkney, promised that they would fly up for the occasion – and what an occasion it was. It was a day of gladness, of a colourful procession of crooks and mitres and blue veils, with joyful strains of festal song sweeping the air as we swung from the byre-chapel down the track to the piece of land on the cliff. Sheep stared at the spectacle bemused and then in panic chased across the field. From then onwards the fund gained ground too. Now the foundations were in place and soon, soon, please God, our home would be built.

The terrain was uneven, despite the levelling work that had been done. There had been a large pond covering most of a deep indentation and for years this had reflected the skies. Now its liquid contents spilled from between towers of sharply contoured blocks, stepped up into the first stages of forming the boat-shaped house and chapel. Weaving in and out of the masonry, I hopped over a dozen puddles that no longer mirrored the firmament as before but instead fractured it into a million multicoloured hues. Then, perching on one of the boulders, I breathed in the scene and the mildness of the air. A flock of oystercatchers settled a stone's throw away and stalked inquisitively back and forth, bobbing up a slope of pasture that a little earlier had been a haze of squill. I squeezed my eyes against the sun, enjoying the meadow now transformed with wild orchids and tormentil.

In Shetland it was a treat to sit outside feeling so warm and I ran a hand gently over the contours of my stone seat. Recently I had chosen another boulder out of this great scattering that had been blasted out of the ground during the levelling process, and had had it deposited a few yards higher up the site. There I had uprighted it myself with a bar, cemented it firmly into place and surrounded it with soil, the idea being that around it we would eventually create a garden. The stone, Lark's Stane, was finger-shaped or perhaps to be

Lark's Stane, before Lark's Hame was built

— 77 —

more accurate, pear-shaped. Now, like a sentinel, it pointed jaggedly into the sky.

Settling myself into a more comfortable position on my boulder, I thought through the past few months. Truly they had been busy, yet also creative in so many ways. There had been Sister Mary Aidan's clothing ceremony in the byre-chapel, an event that we were glad to have captured on film. The BBC had commissioned a series called *Country Women*, and I had been levered into being one of the six subjects. The documentary about us, SOLI, was beautifully produced and called *The Fetlar Nun*. However, as far as we were concerned, it was a one-off for our archives, and we hoped that future members of SOLI would be able to watch it and say, 'Yes, that is how it really was.' I chortled . . . this would undoubtedly be the case for most of them, if not for our new sister, Mary Aidan. Having found at her clothing service that she had no pleats in her scapular, like the two of us who were professed, she was agonizing that she had 'appeared to the world looking like a giant oatcake!'

Then there had been my 'Mothering', as everyone called it. Bishop Bruce had been up to officiate at the service which again took place in the byre-chapel. At this ceremony my role as Mother of the Society was ratified by an official installation and in the receiving of a crook. Also, as planned, 'Mary' was prefixed to my name so that from that day onwards I became known as Mother Mary Agnes.

Yes, there had been many joys this year, but life is never all of one hue and the darker shades of disappointment and anxiety will always, inevitably, touch us.

We had many a Chapter Meeting, or 'family meeting', over those years and the discussion had mostly been focused around Sister Mary Aidan and whether we should continue to keep her at Da Gaets. It was very much her wish, as well as ours, that she should continue there, since in a quiet way she had become something of a 'presence' on the Westside. Indeed, she had become a good friend of all her sparsely scattered neighbours; people recognized her on the local bus going to town and now smiled and spoke. She was able to discuss the snooker game she had seen snatches of on her out-of-the-ark television the night before, or she would share the difficulties of negotiating the steps on the Westside bus when encumbered with shopping. Also, and rather wonderfully, housewives were now coming to Da Gaets for quiet days. Slowly she was being seen as a person with whom everyone could relate, and consequently 'accepted'. However, that did not alter the fact that we had some enormous practical as well as financial difficulties to surmount with regard to the house.

The property did not belong to SOLI, repairs were constantly needed which could not be afforded and the place was isolated with no transportation. Only by calling a taxi could one reach the nearest bus stop several miles away and we had recently discovered that the taxi service itself was to cease. It would then become almost impossible to shop from such a place without owning a car. However, again and again we came back to the reality that her life there in the Culswick valley was of value. Truly, what would have been the point of having struggled this far if we were not going to pursue what had been started with so much faith? Throughout, my own gut feeling remained unchanged . . . somehow we had to overcome all the difficulties, hold tight and keep her there. Rosemary, understanding my feelings, ended one such meeting with a characteristically strong remark.

'Well, I think that if we take her away now, it'll be like an abortion.' She was right. We humans rarely see the whole picture, though in this instance we trusted sufficiently and understood enough to know that we should, unequivocally, accept that 'all things' do 'work together for good to those who love God'. This we did, and were assured beyond doubt that whatever our situation, and wherever it took us, and however perplexing it might be, always that same Love would emanate from the heart.

Now, I thought, standing up, I must wend my way back to The Ness, for Sister Mary Clare would be wondering where on earth I was. Also, there were a few ends to tie up with regard to my journey to the Shetland Mainland on the morrow.

The following day, after an early lunch, I stacked Sybil's suitcase into the back of the car. After bidding farewell to Sister Mary Clare, Rosemary and Frances, Sybil and I set off. Half an hour later, still sitting in the car, we leaned our heads against the seats, closed our eyes and enjoyed the motion of the sea. It was good to let go, especially since I knew that Sybil was as drowsy as I was and that we had at least three-quarters of an hour before we needed to drive off the boat and on to Yell.

Despite this welcome lull, my mind whirred around. Sybil had come up to Shetland earlier in the year for the clothing service of Sister Mary Aidan and was here now for this present occasion of my installation. She had loved the celebrations but on this latest visit had dropped a bombshell, which had caused us a great disappointment. Her doctor had told her that it would be foolish of her to live in such a remote place as Fetlar, where she could not easily get to a hospital. 'Go and live in Shetland, on the Mainland by all means, Sybil, but for goodness' sake, don't land yourself on an isolated island.'

'But what about Weatherhead?' I had cried. Now, several discussions later, I was still trying to reassure our friend that the medical care on Fetlar was both reliable and good. Nevertheless, we couldn't deny the fact that it had taken hours to get her to the hospital after she had slipped and broken her wrist the previous Christmas.

Sybil herself, now silent, was distressed to think that she would not after all be moving to Fetlar, yet it was enormously important to her that she should follow her doctor's advice and not take such a foolish risk. Doctor or no doctor, however, I myself could not shake off the feeling that God, as well as SOLI, needed her here. Despite thinking in this way, we had taken Sybil's circumstances thoroughly on board, and during her visit, we had driven unflaggingly around the Shetland Mainland searching for other possible properties or pieces of land for sale. Finally, even I had begun to persuade myself that, after all, she was meant to live somewhere near to Sister Mary Aidan as a Companion, sharing the life and the Offices and helping her especially with transportation. Therefore we had looked at several houses on the Westside . . . interestingly, with each and every one there had been some reason to turn aside.

So Sybil's stay with us was nearing its end, having seemingly achieved nothing. Now, on this last night, we were staying with Sister Mary Aidan at Da Gaets, and I was to drive her to the airport the next day.

'Don't worry, Mother,' she said, several hours later, as we wound down through the Culswick valley, 'it will all come right.' Abruptly, I pulled on to the verge of the narrow road. The sky was overcast and the light fading. Drizzle dripped down the windows and Sybil glanced at me in surprise.

'Sybil, despite everything that we've considered, how would you like to have a sort of flat in the new house?'

I waited. The silence became protracted . . . Then, putting a hand briefly on mine, she murmured, 'Thank you . . . I'll think about it, Mother.' Quietly I pulled out on to the tarmac.

Da Gaets was warm, with welcoming whiffs of supper in the air when we arrived. Somehow it looked cheerier than usual and we were greeted not only by Sister but also by a small tortoiseshell cat called Pippin. She wound her slim anatomy around our legs, peered into our bags and pranced on and off the furniture, before bouncing on to the table and finally landing on a deep-set windowsill where she stared at us for as long as she could bear to sit still. As we enjoyed supper a while later, Sister Mary Aidan told Sybil the story of her new tortoiseshell friend.

The emaciated creature was seen one morning sitting on the windowsill. Sister had stared, and the tiny cat had stared back, until the feline, satisfied that she had been thoroughly observed, dashed away. Cleverly though, and Pippin is a clever one, her flight took her no more than a stone's throw away, and there she crouched in a patch of overgrowth, peering unflinchingly at Sister's porch door. A saucer of milk was placed invitingly by the door. Predictably and with breakneck speed, the cat not only drank it all but with astonishing boldness stepped into the property to take possession. That night she slept in a corner of Sister's bedroom – not on the bed, for Aros, the cat that Sister Mary Clare had brought back from Canada and who at that time presided at Da Gaets, was very much the steely-eyed queen of the bed.

We could no more have turned Pippin from our door than we could have ignored her equally needy brother, whom the tiny cat had kept alive through her hunting. Barnabas was only introduced, of course, after Pippin had herself secured our undying fidelity. So Pippin, quite a madam, and Barnabas the runt, who has since grown into an elephant-sized softie, were taken for a trip to the vet and subsequently became members of SOLI.

Sybil and I set off the next morning and were driving out

of the valley when she took me by surprise by asking if I would again pull over to the side of the road. This time there was something she needed to ask. Steering on to a flat piece of ground alongside our peat banks, I stopped and turned to face her. She was smiling and could hardly wait to tell me. 'Mother, I hardly slept a wink last night for thinking and thinking, and when I woke up this morning I knew the answer . . . for my mind was quite lucid. I know now that Fetlar's absolutely right for me. Don't ask how – but I know what God is asking . . .'

'There, I told you that Da Gaets has a funny way of making things clear, didn't I?'

'Well, it did last night, and I can tell you, without the slightest doubt, that I've found the way forward. So, if you'll accept me . . . well, I'd like to accept your offer of sharing Lark's Hame.'

I love the cosiness of winter here in Shetland. Its outward darkness is relieved by its inner light and warmth, the crackle of fire being spat up chimneys, and now that oil-fired heating has come to these isles, the comfortable drone of a boiler. One seeks to capture the comfort of such things during these months and to clasp it close as the vigour of our storms increase.

Both cats continued to sleep, despite the fact that I had got up and been to the kitchen and back. Surprisingly I had managed to wiggle my legs down the bed between them again without disturbance. Now, sipping a hot drink, I bundled my pillow more firmly behind my back and allowed my mind to leap to the more temperate climes I had known in the south, and particularly to the nun who had once been my Reverend Mother. Many a time she had related to me a story, a tale from her youth in Cornwall, of how, in her growing understanding of being called to become a religious, she had been given a vision.

One particular winter's night she had been walking along a tree-lined lane to her cottage in the small village where she lived. A young Cornish friend was with her and as was their wont each evening they had said Evensong in the parish church. As they strode along the inexplicable happened – the cold night air was shot with glory and there above them was a globe of light. Rooted to the spot, they stared until gradually, as their pulses calmed, they saw that the light appeared to be in the form of a woman.

From that moment a wonderful vocation began to develop, a vocation to follow our Lord Jesus Christ along a particular path. The nun herself has now long since passed on to glory . . . but her calling continues to unfold in the lives of others.

Again I twitched my legs more comfortably and continued to muse upon the story. Both a theologian and a mystic of that decade believed that this vision had been of Our Lady of Light, of 'a woman clothed with the sun and with the moon under her feet'.

Placing my mug on the chest of drawers by my bed, I groped around for a box of matches and lit a candle, as the electricity had finally spat itself out. Yes, I thought, rearranging myself and returning to my drink, those of us who live on such an isle as Fetlar, far from the city's glare of street lighting, know what darkness means, especially when the moon wanes or is concealed behind cloud. During my first days on Fetlar, I was warned never to leave the house in winter without a torch. Indeed, on the only occasion I ever forgot, my experience served as an excellent reason why it was such a necessity!

We have several feasts of light during the Church's year – a Service of Light in Advent, and of course Candlemas in February. Shetland too revels in light during the dark month of January by celebrating Up-Helly-A. My candle spluttered and I thought again of the nun and of how her community still celebrates the feast of Our Lady of Light in November, on the anniversary of their founder's vision. This also happens to be the *same day that the process for my coming to Shetland was put into place, and since SOLI became official we have kept our own patronal festival of Our Lady of the Isles on that same day, 21 November.*

Sister Mary Aidan has now been given the dedication to Our Lady of Light . . . the light so precious to us here in these dark windswept isles; the light that leads us forward, showing us the way . . . the light that illumines our lives, bringing new horizons to our feet. Light . . . every kind of light, from torchlight's tiny shaft of radiance, to sunlight, which brings warmth and light to the world. Also, of course, there is Mary, Christ's mother, Our Lady of Light . . . and the light that shines in the eyes of every mother able to share her own unique capacity for love. Greatest of all there is Christ, who is the light of all light – who is Light itself and from whom comes that divine spark which glimmers in the heart of us all.

9

Harmonies of Heaven and Earth

A tear rolled down my cheek and surreptitiously I brushed it away with the tip of a finger. We were standing around the Lark's Stane in the raised garden that had begun to develop on the site of our new home on the headland. 'In the name of the Father and of the Son and of the Holy Spirit,' said the clergyman. His alb flapped in the breeze and bowing his head he continued to pray...

Colin and his wife Barbara, both SOLI Caim members, were staying with us and he, an Anglican priest, had kindly suggested that we say a few relevant prayers for our doggie friend, Tildy. Tildy, short for Matilda, was appropriately an Australian terrier who had belonged to Sister Mary Clare and her late husband during their years abroad. Joining SOLI after she was widowed, Mary Clare had brought her pets along too, so they had seen her through many vicissitudes. During the last few years of Tildy's life on Fetlar I also had grown to love her, and looking now at the small bundle through a screen of tears I watched Colin place her into the petal-lined pit that we had dug by the standing stone. The rough face of the stone out of which I had chiselled a Celtic cross spoke volumes, while Colin, comfortingly and in his easy manner, spoke to us of Tildy's unique place in God's creation.

Moments later Sister Mary Clare waving an arm called out, 'Now, is everyone ready? Awaaay then! Let them all go.'

A light breeze caught up a flotilla of balloons, one for each year of the little dog's life. They rose, each bandying with the other for supremacy of flight and each a token of love for the four-legged friend whose name Sister had written across them. 'Thank you Tildy', were simple enough words, yet for her on that grey afternoon they stabbed both the heart and mind with memories and meaning.

On the telephone that evening I described the scene to Sybil and she asked if we would ever consider replacing Tildy. 'Well,' I said, 'as you're aware, there's hardly room in The Ness for Sister Mary Clare, the cats and me, and as you can imagine Skerry, Flugga and Mooskit aren't going to take kindly to the idea of another dog, especially if the dog's a puppy. Tildy had been ideal, she was such a gentle and undemanding little creature . . . No, Sybil, it's not exactly what I'd choose. Though actually,' and here I lowered my voice, 'Sister's already mentioned the subject!' Looking around and easing the phone more comfortably against my ear I went on to tell her what Sister felt. 'She thinks that it would be a good thing to have a puppy, now, while we're still living in the croft house . . . so as to train it before we move into the new house.' Then I dared to ask our friend the leading question. 'Sybil, you're going to be living in Lark's Hame with us, how do you feel about another dog?'

'Oh, Mother, I love dogs, and I agree with Sister. If we are having one, then it ought to be trained before we move into the house. By the way, have you heard when the builders are coming?'

I laughed. 'Sybil, while the builders were here a few months ago working on the foundations, they said that they'd start on the structural part of the building as soon as possible.

Remember? "We'll work through the summer, Sister," they said, "so as to get the whole thing completed before the winter." And guess what, there hasn't been any sight or sound of them since. We're horribly disappointed, and of course before we know it, we'll be hurtling towards our bad weather spell again. Never mind, how is it going at your end of things, re the house sale, I mean?'

Excitedly, Sybil explained that there was a possibility of a church friend buying her house, 'and there's something else that's going to please you, Mother, it's amazing really. It's that my doctor's just read your first book and tells me that it's caused her to change her whole opinion about my coming to Fetlar . . . she's now suggesting that I, well, that I, "go for it"!'

'Gosh!'

'Yes, I'm so happy, Mother. I knew that my decision at Da Gaets was right. You see, I felt quite certain that it was God speaking to me. I told you that, didn't I?'

'Yes, Sybil, you did . . .'

So the weeks of June, our Shetland month of constant light both day and night, came and went. Sybil sold her house in Reading and life leapt onwards, though still without sign of the builders. As always, there was a series of occurrences, one concerning Sister Mary Aidan, who was called to the hospital in Aberdeen to have a cataract operation.

It was while Sister and I were south, for I accompanied her myself to the great city, that Shuna, a cross-German shepherd bitch, bounced into our lives. Sister Mary Clare had rung the Grampian dog sanctuary and arranged for a puppy to be brought to the Aberdeen home of the friends with whom we were staying. The idea was that we should either take this one or that I should say a definite no to having any dog. Psychologically this was an excellent move on Sister's part, for the whole thing, a foregone conclusion, was in the bag as soon as the dog appeared. One glance into the appealing eyes of this golden-haired stray with her black muzzle and large feet was enough to convince us. Immediately, I was practically grovelling to sign the necessary papers and to

Shuna

arrange with the sanctuary for the pup to be flown north. In a comparatively short time she was popped into a box and on to the plane and there, at the Shetland end, Sister Mary Clare was ready and waiting to take her in hand.

After Sister Mary Aidan's operation, she and I boarded a train and spent a fortnight in a holiday house lent to us by friends in the Lake District. Here we lapped up the sunshine, enjoyed seeing trees again and breathed in Wordsworth. Also we met up with Paddy, the producer of the *Country Women* film, with whom I was to do my last bits of 'voice-over'. After this, we joyfully returned home feeling, as always, that it was worth every moment of being away for the sheer pleasure of returning.

Months skidded past and eventually tumbled into autumn. With the long nights of the 'Simmer Dim' well behind us, we found ourselves preparing for Sybil's permanent arrival. By this time we had divided the interior of Weatherhead, having come to the conclusion that the property was far too large for Frances to occupy on her own. Happily, and at her initiation, one side of it had now become her home, and the other used as extra visitor accommodation. It was here that Sybil was to reside temporarily. She settled in with rejoicing, and for a few weeks they were joined in the house by an American lady from Boston, Massachusetts.

Jean, in her early sixties, was tall, dark-haired and full of smiles. These attributes, plus her enormous energy, gave her an incredibly youthful appearance. She had visited us for a long weekend earlier in the year and we had all instantly sensed that God had a plan! We talked, laughed and listened and she would have stayed longer . . . However, she departed after her two days to continue her planned itinerary through Britain. We had agreed that as she travelled onwards we would all ponder upon God's will of whether she should return to us a few weeks later. The result of our prayers was that Jean was now back to spend most of October and November on Fetlar before flying home to the States.

During her initial visit, I had a couple of times walked with our new friend around the foundations of Lark's Hame. Now she was to share the real excitement of the project with us, for as it worked out the builders also arrived in October. Since our long months of winter gales often set in and could blow up quite viciously by this time of the year, the weather had to be most carefully monitored by the builders. The house and chapel had arrived, in kit form, on the back of two huge lorries. Now, with bated breath, we listened to every weather forecast, praying for the calm days needed to erect the structure. Our Shetland days were, by now, shortening at strapping pace.

Despite our fears with regard to the time of year, the builders had chosen their first week well and within a few days the skeleton of Lark's Hame was standing, silhouetted on the headland. The days now, as well as the nights, were dark and apart from a few hours in every 24, the builders worked by floodlight. The structure rose, suddenly appearing to the isle like a giant illuminated ark. Keeping our binoculars by the skylight of my bedroom in The Ness, I strained to see every bit of progress. It was with deep longing that I looked and waited now to see the building finished. Amazingly soon, we could, after years of dreaming and planning, move into it and make it our 'home'. Indeed, this house was going to provide us with the space we so desperately needed as well as allow us the privilege of at last releasing The Ness for the use of novices.

So, the whole concept of our boat-shaped home grew and through one miracle after another and after much prayer it was at last appearing. Although it is only a one-and-a-half-storey dwelling, with its upper floor in the roof, the building might look to some people to be far too imposing for SOLI, more imposing than it really is. Its deceptive appearance is caused mostly by the fact that it stands on the edge of the cliff and also by our having had a small chapel added to the east gable, which gives it length.

We enjoyed Jean's stay with us and even celebrated Thanksgiving Day for the first time in our English lives. We hung balloons and prepared a surprise meal, mainly to help her to feel less homesick on such a festive American family day.

So, Jean's second stint with SOLI passed quickly and during that time we ascertained that she felt called to join us, with the hope of testing her vocation as a Sister. However, she needed to return to the States for a year, to reflect on her hopes from afar and also to think upon how her two sons, in their early twenties, would be affected by the move and would fit into the overall picture. Ultimately, she would need to sell her house and settle her affairs. We also needed our own time of deliberation and discernment and, as is always the case, our own time too of preparation, in order to open not only the door of our community but also the doors of our hearts. Everyone who is truly sent here needs to be made room for, welcomed and ultimately allowed to add a new dimension to the life and its purpose.

Sadly the day came for us to say farewell to Jean and on a wintry night when the cold ate into one's marrow we squeezed into the car and trailed to the ferry. Waves whipped the pier, tossing and hissing over a conglomeration of gigantic boulders. A jumbled arm of the same great rocks had been bulldozed into a protecting promontory and within the scant embrace of this seemingly indomitable wall, the boat would soon dock. Out at sea all was blackness, bar the wink of a green starboard light drawing closer. Then, with the deck-lights suddenly up, the vessel flared into view, into being. Magically it appeared, swirling forward towards us, scattering fountains of brilliance. Eventually, coupled to the dock, the roar of its engine rattled into the whoosh of the waves, while the boat, as though with a mind of its own, continuously rose and fell. Heaving and stretching against its fetters, it creaked open its visor. We clambered from the car and after hugs and final adieus, helped Jean on to the deck. Resignedly she pushed her baggage under cover and leaned against the deck-rail, illuminated for a moment in a glare of floodlight. The coldness bit deeper and after a final flick of her hand she ducked in through a door and disappeared from sight. We, reluctant to leave, climbed to a drier vantage point, getting colder by the minute. After what seemed like a lifetime of waiting the small ship, its few passengers now on board, throbbed violently into life. The ramp rose, snapped itself shut and the vessel lurched forward, spewing another flux of glistening ripples across the water and leaving behind it a trail of brilliance – and a motley trail of waving women. Mischievously, the skipper honked the boat's horn, causing us to jump sky-high, and then dipped its lights. Shivering, I groped for my torch and we hurried to the car. The boat's bulk, with now only the faintest wink of a port light to prove its existence, was being sucked into the night.

The night took its course and I, companioned by the cats, continued to think upon life. Yesterday, before the storm, I had paused as on many occasions before the pointed recess window of this room, now familiarly known as 'Mother's room'. West facing, the panes of glass reach from the floor to a low apex ceiling and the sensation when looking outwards is of standing high in the prow of a ship, looking from a place where one has not just the world but the universe cast at one's feet. Standing or sitting in this place is a feast of beauty, a holy feast when one devours a scene constantly calling to be savoured in every mood, in its every disclosure of a reality beyond and yet intrinsically a part of itself. Daily I could now look out on a cosmos spinning out the story of life itself, with its blue seas and sunshine, its grey days, its stillness, its violent storms and its sparkling canopy of stars. From here I could embrace the aurora borealis, the 'merry dancers', fluttering and skipping through a winter's night and floodlighting the northern sky. I could gaze at the ocean cast around our Aithness point, overhung and illuminated by the moon, the moon that is so companionable one minute and so elusive another. The dear solitary moon, the moon that had been so great a friend of mine throughout my solitary years, as it swung across its own vast seas untouched by chaos and dispelling the darkness of our poor fearful world.

Yes, here from this window there would always be peace, and on the dullest days a hint of brilliance – a shining, that comes from the source of all shining. A shining that can be seen in the whole of God's creation and in his lovers; a shining that is a jewel beyond price for all those who have the eyes to see.

Yesterday I had stood, as I shall stand many times more, my eyes riveted over the deep blue-greens of the water, and I had traced the half-mile curve of Tresta Bay on the glass. The sun had been painting the beach, a ribbon of gold across the canvas, and brushing the hills with light. At that moment it was impossible to imagine a heaven more beautiful. Yet I knew that it was and that the picture before me was no more than a blink of its glory. I knew also that in this reflection of heaven one could understand better the bond between all that is and all that will be. Truly, this window was a place of passing from one realm to another where divisions melt, colours merge and contrasts complement and enhance. Indeed, it is always here, standing on the edge of a mystery that can draw one into itself and where one can stretch out one's arms to receive its gift, that we too are asked to give . . . This is so, for it is only in the act of giving as well as in receiving that love can be consummated and heaven grasped.

In the knowing of this truth, I was conscious of that woman clothed with the sun and with the moon under her feet who seemed to say, 'He is the everliving God, the eternal Christ and he is in you and in whoever takes of his body and blood.'

A certain anchoress by the name of Mother Ivy at the beginning of the twentieth century said, 'Our Lord's body and blood fill the universe.' We, in our standing before Christ as empty vessels, *willing to receive and willing to give, become receptacles also of all that we behold. We become bearers of beauty – bearers of Christ and are transformed into who we truly are.*

The eastern aspect of the new house is different from and yet similar to the west, especially as we stoop through a small door out on to a gallery, which overhangs our octagonal-shaped chapel. Here, high under the beams of the roof, one can see across the chapel. One can see over the altar and on out through yet another window, the east window, this time to the garden, to the distant hills and to a line of sea, to a sea that this night is tossed and shaken in darkness. Yet there is always a tomorrow, when the storm is over . . . Then one can not only peer but step into this holy place, this place of worship, this place of the Eucharist, this place of the body and the blood of our Lord Jesus Christ, this place of a great mystery:

Come, 'take of the Bread and drink of the Wine . . .'

10

Surging Seas

When Lark's Hame was completed we had barely enough money to live on without having to think about the furnishing of the new chapel. Nevertheless, since we had already arranged a date with the Bishop when he would come up to Shetland to bless and dedicate the building, basic furniture was required quickly. Folk were coming from far and near to share the celebrations and some of the more elderly would need to sit down, so seating was the priority. The old bench table from the but room in The Ness would make an altar, and we had a spare pair of candlesticks in the byre-chapel.

During my early days on Fetlar I had turned the byre into a chapel by making all the benches and pews myself. One could not deny, however, that my efforts, although adequate, were rustic. The more I studied my designs for the new chapel the more I realized that my carpentry was not sophisticated enough to manage the job on my own. There was also the question of money for the buying of the necessary wood. Happily, the latter problem was surmounted by Sybil, who saved the day by organizing a sponsorship effort.

Marvellously, and with little time left before the great day descended, I received a letter from one of our Caim members. In her note, Jill was reminding me of something she had suggested to me a few months earlier. With mounting pleasure, I found that the whole gist of her missive was that if we needed anything making for the new chapel, her husband Hugh, a retired farmer whose hobby was carpentry, would be delighted to help. 'Anything,' she said, 'would be a challenge to him, be it a prayer-desk, candlesticks or whatever.'

'Wonderful,' I shouted, waving the sheets of notepaper at Sister Mary Clare. Knowing that there was not a moment to lose, I rang Jill. The end result was that this generous couple packed their camper van with a selection of tools, boarded the *St Clair* in Aberdeen and in due course arrived at our chapel door to teach me carpentry.

Life does not always work out as planned, and the week that Jill and Hugh were with us a hundred and one other things tumbled to the fore. The electricians arrived to finish the wiring – centred in the chapel; the carpet people arrived to fit the carpets – in the chapel. If that was not enough, a huge Pickfords van loaded with Sybil's furniture from Reading thundered to a halt outside.

Hugh, spreading my drawings before him, wasted no time in working out the exact measurements of wood needed. Then, while the carpet was being laid and the lighting fixed, he and I travelled to the Shetland Mainland to buy planks, screws, sandpaper and tacks.

During their stay, Hugh and I made most of the bench seating around the octagonal-shaped chapel. We also worked on two or three of the kneeling-desks. He showed me how to construct properly in wood and how to use some of his excellent equipment. The altar design he decided to take home with him and craft that very special piece of furniture in his own workshop. We were thrilled with our efforts. Having learned so much more about carpentry I was determined to complete the task myself the following winter. This I actually managed to do, making more desks and seating, and achieving the lovely circular effect I had hoped for. I wanted it to reflect our Lord's own encompassing. However, despite our good progress, there is still work to be done and I am definitely planning a period of creativity when my present task of writing is accomplished.

Nevertheless, by the day of the chapel blessing and the arrival of the Bishops and Father Lewis, the choir from St Magnus in Lerwick and all our guests, there was seating for everyone.

After our move into Lark's Hame, we left The Ness sitting empty for several months. This saddened me deeply, especially seeing its increasing air of dejection, but by October, when we knew for certain that Jean was returning, I felt cheered. Soon the little house would be loved into life again.

We polished, scrubbed and moved furniture around from here to there and at last stood back to view our handiwork. The Ness needed all sorts of renovation that we could not afford, but at least we had made it look welcoming and comfortable. The plan was that Jean should settle into this little croft-house that was so especially dear. Probably she would stay there, but first we had to ascertain where the future was leading us with regard to her call. Taking into consideration that she had sons still in the States, we first needed to be quite sure that she was going to settle peacefully. 'Home', for her, was many miles away and although her family were all fairly grown-up, a mother is always a mother.

Our process of discernment at that time was quite a stiff one in as much as it demanded that the aspirant should wait a whole year before coming to Fetlar. This had been the procedure for Sister Mary Clare and we had felt at the time that it was a good one. So the idea was that on top of this initial year of thinking and praying about things, the aspirant, if still of the same mind, would go forward into a year of living alongside. Our timing for Jean's arrival was spot-on, for joyfully she landed during our preparations for Sister Mary Clare's Profession of Vows.

Sister Mary Clare was the first of those sent to me to reach the stage of making a full life commitment and this made the occasion of her Life Profession most especially moving. Also on this, her day, we were celebrating SOLI's patronal festival of Our Lady of the Isles. Again, the Bishop flew up to Shetland to officiate and Sister Mary Clare, presented to him to make her vows, was consecrated to Mary's Holy Son, to Jesus Christ her Lord, and was given a dedication that would become uniquely hers. Most Sisters at Life Vows are given a dedication. Mine, long ago in Devon, was to Our Lady of Joy, and I personally had hoped that our first SOLI Sister could be given the dedication to Our Lady of Light. This would have seemed appropriate for Sister Mary Clare in several ways, and most particularly since 'Clare' signifies light. However, in the end she had a choice of two dedications and she chose 'Jesus the Good Shepherd'.

Sister's profession was glorious, for it was a giving of her whole life to God in the manner in which she believed he was asking of her. Kneeling before Bishop Bruce, in the new chapel of Christ the Encompasser, she promised to live in the poverty of love, in the obedience of love and in the purity of love, which is how SOLI interprets the vows. Solemnly she promised these things with the intention of serving her Lord for the rest of her life as a SOLI Sister:

> 'I Sister Mary Clare, of Jesus the Good Shepherd
> and member of this family of the Society of Our Lady
> of the Isles, promise to the best of my ability and with
> God's help, to walk in the way of Jesus the Good
> Shepherd. And now in the presence of you, Bishop Bruce
> of Aberdeen and Orkney, you Canon Lewis Smith our
> Warden, you Mother Mary Agnes and you my sisters
> and friends, I offer and bind myself to Almighty God
> and vow that in every aspect of my life and to the end
> of my days I will walk in his love . . .'

After the profession, Bishop Bruce and Father Lewis stayed on for a few days. They both thought it an excellent idea to make this opportunity of being together a chance to talk about SOLI's future. This being so, the Bishop drew up a schedule to cover the three days and he called our conference, 'Focus for the Future'.

Admittedly we were all tired, though I do not use that as an excuse for my fractiousness during the dialogue of those ensuing three days; anything that savours of whirling God into our own recipes for life instead of allowing him to bind us into his I abhor. Therefore, I have to confess that it was extremely difficult to sit in my allotted group discussing what I thought were complex trivialities. However, having said that, I have to add that I hold our Bishop in the highest esteem and know that this is the slow, careful route along which the Church often has to proceed. Nevertheless, on this occasion I felt increasingly frustrated. Why did we have to make God's call so complicated? Why not just live it out in the straightforward and joyful way that he had asked of us? Wasn't that the reason he had brought me to this tiny island in the first place? Indeed, discussions and talking about our life, taking it to pieces and putting it together again, felt like a waste of energy and it was all far too political for me. The first day passed slowly, and what to me was God's gloriously simple vision for SOLI and its future lay fractured, labelled and compartmentalized and, worst of all, my spiritual family seemed to be relishing the sessions!

By the end of the second day I was bursting with indignation and that night, unable to sleep, I uncharacteristically got up, pulled out the elderly computer and hammered away at its keys, hurling my thoughts on to paper. This was how I saw SOLI's focus for the future. It was all so simple really... could be held in a nutshell... Suddenly, feeling more than a little shocked at myself, I smiled, relaxing. Gracious, what amazingly violent means 'hurt' can cause one to use, especially for the purpose of trying to jump things back into focus. I stopped typing. Well, Christ had done it... he had jolted things back into perspective, hadn't he, when he'd tipped up the tables in the temple? Many times when I have been looking at life, mostly other people's, I have seen that it is 'pain' that so often bounces us forward, into actions we might never have taken.

The next day at our first session I read my paper, and a new spiritual chapter for SOLI began... though that is another book!

The storm had taken a new hold, thrashing the south front of the house with renewed vigour. Trying hard to occupy my mind with other thoughts, I began to relive that private conversation I had shared with our Bishop and Warden, after our 'Focus for the Future' time together.

'I always knew that this would happen,' Father Lewis had laughed.

His remark, which had no connection whatever with our conference sessions, had surprised me. He had been a good friend of mine since I had landed on Shetland's shores a decade earlier, and he well knew my views on the topic that had been introduced out of the blue. It was the ordination of women and I had, after all, come from a very traditional religious-life background.

'I'm only saying,' I had stammered, a little taken aback, 'that it's just a pity that SOLI can never have the Eucharistic Prayer unless there's a visiting priest here, which is almost never. No, no, of course I wasn't thinking about ordination for myself... Of course not...'

Living over 50 miles and two ferry journeys away from Father Lewis, our nearest priest, meant that our eucharistic services for ourselves, our guests and neighbours were always set around the receiving of our communion from the Reserved Sacrament. These occasions were unquestionably precious, especially since we had made them as perfect as we could by including the use of beautiful church music. Yet, the omission of the Eucharistic Prayer, this vital and most important part of the liturgy, was an enormous deprivation.

Bishop Bruce and Father Lewis had been sitting here in this very room. They had looked at me quietly and waited. Flustered, and I did not know why, I found myself launching headlong into the place of no return. Distinctly I heard Mother Mary Agnes's voice – mine – rattling on, yet could not extricate her. It was as though I was listening to someone else ... I could hear my own voice telling them how we as a community had collected together a couple of years before to listen to the Church of England debates regarding the ordination of women. Yes, and of how towards the end of the transmission when the voting took place I had suggested that we also take a vote, basically to make clear where we stood as a community. Since we are used to being honest with each other, all happily acquiesced and as I looked for the paper and pencils, I presumed, not a little smugly, that I knew exactly how the result would fall. I would say a definite 'no', Sister Mary Clare would say an absolute 'yes', and Rosemary a 'well, so long as I'm dead when it happens,' and so on . . .

Silently, the men listened, allowing me to talk on. I explained that the result of SOLI's vote had stunned us all, for it had been a unanimous 'yes'!

That night in bed I struggled to work out why I, personally, had felt so compelled to write 'yes', and in a flash it came to me. It was, I decided, because I believed that we are all of us a part of the royal priesthood. Then, in a later flash, I realized that what I had so disliked and had said no, no, no, to was not the actual ordination of women but the then rampant feminist attitude surrounding the issue. Indeed, what I had really disliked about women being ordained was the striving of some of them to be like the men, instead of remaining true to themselves.

Now, in bed on this stormy night, my thoughts rolled around, while Flugga, noticing that I was awake, had tumbled up the bed and was sitting beside my pillow. Placing a gentle paw on my head and with slightly extended claws, he tugged my hair.

'Ouch! Not now, Flugga,' I said, 'go to the bottom of the bed – food later.'

Yes, I remembered, I had been just as awake during that night of deliberation, after the Synod debate on the ordination of women and then, at that later date, passing on my findings to the men.

'You see,' I remembered saying to them, 'it all suddenly became clear, for I came upon the perfect way of explaining it . . . to myself, I mean. It was so lucid and so simple really, for I realized that the Sacrament itself symbolized everything . . . that the chalice represented the female and the paten the male. Put the two together and there was the perfect whole.'

Yes, I had thought excitedly, why hadn't someone understood this before? A female, in herself, was mysteriously linked to the cup, to that Holy Grail, she was the shape, the vessel, she was the chalice, the bearer of Christ. Then there was sacrificial blood too . . . yes . . . The male role was different and was meant to be so in order that, brought together, they might create wholeness, might be made one, might complement each other fully and strongly in their showing forth of Christ.

Mooskit was tramping up the bed now. He was such a lump, and no doubt he was hungry too. Pressing the light switch I found that the power was still off. 'Moosy, you'll just have to wait.'

Now, a few years after Synod's decision to ordain women, I thank God for my own glorious priesthood and for all that it means . . .

So many priests are weighed up and given marks out of ten for being good leaders or good preachers, and occasionally I think for being good pray-ers. Yet none of these things is so vital as being able to show forth Christ. None is so important as being a good channel of Love. How constantly we who are priests need to ask ourselves one question: are we so selfless, so thinly transparent that our flock can see right through us to Christ? If so, then we are fulfilling our role. If our flock can, indeed, see through us to Christ, whose body and blood we hold on the paten and in the chalice, we are fulfilling our call.

There was a sudden lull in the storm, and as it hung, as it were, suspended, I saw in my mind's eye – Our Lady holding a chalice . . .

11
Strains of Solitude

The November days darkened and the wind grew louder. One afternoon Bob the postman left a remarkable letter among the pile on the hall chest. It was from a lady who had just read my first book. Her correspondence, which later was to set off a whole series of events, told of her excitement in having possibly hit upon a shared link with me in the past. I had written into my book an account of my sister Carole's 'healing'. 'I'd be so interested to learn who the "old" priest was who visited your sick baby sister,' she said in her letter. As an infant Carole had been cured of pneumonia through the ministrations of the parish priest of our small Nottinghamshire village.

Flipping through the sheets of paper, I became fascinated by the content of her dissertation and particularly by her questions. 'Was the village where you lived called Old Brinsley? And was the priest's name John Frederick Starmer?' As it turned out her guesses about my childhood background were absolutely correct, for the priest of our village had been her father and, as she went on to explain, he had possessed the gift of healing. Delightedly I wrote back and filled her in and she, equally thrilled, learned that her 'Dad' had in fact married my parents and baptized Carole and me. 'Yes,' I wrote, 'I can see him clearly, he was quite old and had white hair.' Later and with some amusement his daughter, Margaret, enlightened me that he would only have been in his fifties!

This letter, so providential, proved the beginning of a unique friendship, one through which I was privileged to touch both deep and unexpected spiritual dimensions, extraordinarily connected with Our Lady.

Soon after this first interchange of letters with Margaret, our first Christmas card of the season arrived. Running my fingers over the knobbly feel of the envelope, I slit it open and looked inside. There, tucked into the card, was a medallion. Twisting it between finger and thumb to peer more closely, I found it was a medal of Our Lady of Peace. Glancing down at the card, I saw that it was from a priest friend in London, Father Rodney. His writing was bold, telling me that he and his wife Vicki had twice been to Medjugorje, the now well-known Croatian village where Our Lady, Christ's mother, was still appearing to some of the six visionaries. Gosh! I thought, remembering that the appearances had started about the time I had arrived on Fetlar. That would make the apparitions to the children, who must by now have grown into adulthood, at least 14 years in duration. I returned the card to its envelope, still pondering on the priest's words. 'Our visit to this place', he had written, 'has changed our lives . . .'

What little we knew about the Medjugorje story was only what Rosemary who had herself been dedicated to Our Lady of Peace when she had tested her vocation at Posbury, had gleaned. Her information and centre of interest had been entirely related to 'peace'. Often, when leading our intercessions on Fetlar, she had used the lovely prayer for peace given to the children by Our Lady. Interestingly, Mary had told the children her identity, that she was the 'queen of peace', so it was this aspect of Medjugorje that linked Rosemary so solidly with her patron. As for all the other stuff, well, as those of us who had known Rosemary for some years were well aware, being such a down-to-earth sort of person, she was not much given to wild imaginings. She certainly did not like talking about any sort of phenomena.

The third link in this chain of events was that a day or two after the Medjugorje card arrived, Sister Mary Aidan asked me if, on my next visit to Da Gaets, I would bring a fresh selection of books from our library to update her spiritual reading.

'Only on condition that you return the box-full that I brought you to read a year ago,' I said. She had laughed and assured me that she would have the box of books ready. True to her word, it was waiting and we carried it up to the car. It was then that I noticed with enormous surprise that I had actually lent her a book about Medjugorje. It was a slim volume, one that I had not the slightest recollection of ever having seen. Placing it in the car so that it was accessible on my journey home, I snatched it up on the first ferry crossing, clicked on the car light and began to read.

It was a filthy day and by the time I arrived home darkness had long descended. Pulling up outside Lark's Hame, with the windscreen wipers still belting back and forth, I peered into the gloom. At that moment, as if by magic, the vestibule lights flashed on, illuminating a window. 'Good, they've finished saying Vespers,' I thought. A sudden pathway of light was tossed towards me as the chapel door opened and Rosemary's stalwart figure looked out. Switching off the engine I caught snatches of speech and once I was out of the car I saw her macintoshed figure, now marching through the murk towards me.

'I'll give you a hand to empty the car,' she nodded, and in two ticks was making a beeline for the books!

'They're too heavy, Rosemary,' I shouted. 'Here, have something to cover them.'

She had gone deaf to any suggestions – rather conveniently,

I suspected, knowing Rosemary's reputation with regard to books, in order to have a quick peek! Catching a glimpse of her shape pushing in through the back entrance of the house I knew that was the end of any help! Unloading the car myself, I pushed past her several times. She was engrossed in the pages of – the Medjugorje book.

Rain still glistened on her face when, finally shutting the back door, I handed her a towel. She flapped the book at me. 'I say,' she said. 'Let's go – to Medjugorje, shall we?'

Earlier in the year she had suggested that we have a holiday together but somehow the plans for it had aborted. These days I am totally happy to stay at home, which means I am not always very good at arranging or being interested in holidays for myself. So on that occasion, although it could have been fun, I had been quietly relieved that Rosemary seemed to have shelved the idea. Now, however, she was brightly suggesting an alternative. 'D'you know anyone who's been there?' she pressed and I told her about the card I had received from Father Rodney and Vicki. 'Oh, do ring them . . . Go and do it now, Mother,' she hustled me.

'Anything for a quiet life,' I said, limping upstairs with Rosemary in tow. My arthritic spine was apt to play up at the end of a long day and lamed me in one of my legs. However, once upstairs, I sat down, lifted the telephone and dialled Father Rodney's number. Thankfully there was no answer. I grinned at Rosemary and taking off my damp scapular turned to happier thoughts of a meal. 'Well,' she said, ambling off with a determined set to her shoulders, 'we'll try again tomorrow.'

By the next evening I had forgotten Rosemary's insistence that I should ring our priest friend – until, to my great surprise, Sister Mary Clare called me over to the phone.

'It's Father Rodney,' she said.

'No,' he said, 'I had no idea you'd tried to get me last night. Vicki and I were out, and I'm sorry to trouble you now, over supper, but I really do have to talk to you . . . about Medjugorje'!

The long and the short of his call was that he was arranging another pilgrimage and hoped that I would join the party. Knowing that SOLI could in no way rise to the expense of such a holiday, I told him that really it was Rosemary who was interested. Carefully I mentioned nothing at all about costs or of our having no holiday money. Nevertheless he stressed that he would post the information to both of us.

A couple of days later the telephone rang again, and again it was Father Rodney. 'Guess what? I've something quite unbelievable sitting on my desk,' he said.

Of course, having no idea what it could be, I became more surprised by the second. It turned out that a lady in his congregation, who wished to remain anonymous, had given him a cheque to cover all my expenses to Croatia the next year!

Christmas came and went and we began making our preparations for the service in the new chapel when Sister Mary Aidan, still a novice, would be received into Simple Vows. St Bride's Day, the Vigil of Candlemas, dawned bright and calm and we assembled with all our friends to support her in the making of her vows.

Sunlight streamed through the narrow side window on to the veiled figure kneeling before the altar. Although the small octagonal-shaped chapel was full of people and the air was ringing with expectancy, nothing encroached upon that awed stillness of anticipation. Everyone waited, hushed into silence, as Sister Mary Aidan was about to make her Simple or Temporary Vows as they are sometimes called. The priest, slim and tall, with a Shetland dialect, was still young enough to show few signs of the distinguished greying of his hair. He smiled down at the woman before him.

'Sister Mary Aidan, I now invite you to pledge yourself in the service of Christ . . .' His voice rose and fell, asking her to bind herself to Christ, under the threefold vows made by SOLI. This she was invited to do for a period of one year only, at the end of which it was expected that she would be ready to renew her vows for a further year. After three consecutive years she would be invited to make her Life Vows, that is, if elected by a two-thirds majority of favourable votes from the Chapter.

She looked up and then spoke, clearly and without hesitation.

> 'I, Sister Mary Aidan, a member of the Society of Our Lady of the Isles, promise to the best of my ability and with God's help, to bind myself to Christ within the religious life of this community for a period of no less than one year . . .'

Sister Mary Aidan made her vows, those three interweaving cords of love, of the Love who is our God. She made those three promises, entwined within and symbolizing the most Holy Trinity, the Three in One. Firmly she bound herself to the Poverty of Love, the Obedience of Love and the Purity of Love. And so she made these, her first vows. Afterwards came the spadework of cultivating her vocation within that plot of ground that the master gardener called SOLI.

Later, the hitherto unimaginable happened and I made my own first tentative commitment in another direction. The date of my ordination to the diaconate, in St Andrew's Cathedral, Aberdeen, arrived – as did my sister Carole and her husband Eric, along with a wonderful throng of SOLI

Caim members and many friends from far and near. Many times I have recalled the occasion, and recently came across an old newsletter written by Rosemary and which says it all:

Dear friends,
What a lot of news there is to catch up with!

Mother Mary Agnes and I left Fetlar together on 17 June. Mother caught the evening boat to Aberdeen. She was to have a three-day retreat, so I used a different route and had a little jaunt to Orkney. I enjoyed myself exploring new places – visited an old friend – dabbled in a second-hand bookshop – and watched three eider ducks shielding their little families from the dark intentions of a hoodie-crow.

Sisters Mary Clare and Mary Aidan joined

E for eider ducks

Mother and me at the cathedral in Aberdeen on the Saturday evening for the rehearsal. Everything seemed white and dazzling. The whiteness of the walls seemed to extend its outreach. Those of us who were to 'present' the ordinands were given seats at the front of the nave. This meant a long look forward to the sanctuary, but not much connection with the people behind us.

On the Sunday, the day itself – suddenly all the music and the majesty of the occasion came into its own. There was that shining whiteness all around us . . .

I had guessed that Tim's side of the nave would be well supported as he was known locally and had been involved with work at the university. I had expected Mother's friends, Caim members, and family would cling to the first few pews. In a miraculous way, the few turned to many – and the cathedral was packed!

The feeling of togetherness was overpowering. Certainly many more 'joined us in spirit'. Cathedral music stirred and swept us to our feet – and it had begun! The procession came on – onwards and onwards – so much colour and throng! Priests came – university dignitaries – the choir – and finally, the two ordinands and the Bishop himself . . .

Night battered itself onwards towards a dishevelled dawn and I pondered upon so many new beginnings. My ordination had been one such portico in the life of SOLI, and that had opened up new and precious shaping to our lifestyle. From a cosmetic viewpoint we were surrounded by a now beautiful garden. Jean had started the next chapter of her life in the binding of herself to the same commitment as Rosemary and Sybil, as a Companion of SOLI. She had also moved from The Ness into the small hermitage house she had had built at the end of the road to Lark's Hame. Added to this burgeoning, two new and important visitors arrived to stay. The first was a young woman, yet another schoolteacher, by the name of Alison Jackson and the second a retired clergy widow, who turned out to be another Sybil.

Sybil Roebuck had come up to Shetland to share her plans of starting a project in Orkney and to ask for help. She stayed for about a week, during which time Sister Mary Clare became increasingly drawn by Sybil's ideas of forming a small Christian centre on the island of Rousay. Our talk with Sybil culminated in Sister and I departing to Rousay at the end of her stay, to look at the project more closely to see if and how God meant SOLI to fit in.

Over the previous decade, a hermit by the name of David Rawlings, a priest, had lived on Rousay in a caravan, which had been tugged to the top of a hill, interestingly by our friend Hugh when he and Jill had lived in Orkney. There, he and David had sited it in a small quarried-out hollow. The land and seascapes around the hill were magnificent, though the place itself was greatly exposed to the gales. David, experiencing the conditions, built a high wall around his hermitage. Now, after his death, it continues to stand like a beacon – witnessing to the God whom he loved. Sybil and her husband had become great friends with David and after his death, and the death of her husband, Sybil bought the buildings, along with the farmland on which they were situated, with the aim of continuing a life of prayer and work and hospitality.

I came away from Orkney leaving a buoyant Sister Mary Clare for a while longer, though feeling that the only part of the project that was truly SOLI-oriented was the hermitage. SOLI's call was daily becoming clearer to me; in part, it was that of a beacon, a light lit by God and, indeed, set upon a hill. More and more I had begun to realize that out of the clamour of the previous few years of officialdom and growth, our call was to the freedom of a certain type of solitary life. It was to a life unique to SOLI; through the hoped-for giving of each Sister wholly to God, it could attain a transparency through which Christ himself could shine. From its centre he alone could touch the hearts of many.

A hint of daylight touched my skylight, and the poignant words of Our Lady touched my soul:

'Open your heart to him that he may be within all your lives . . .'

12

The Whole Earth Sings

Sister Mary Aidan and I sat in the gloom of the but room at Da Gaets. The first autumn puddle had appeared in one of the loft rooms and Sister had been telling me that she was finding the garden increasingly difficult to handle. 'I don't want to grumble,' she said, 'but life here isn't always easy, you know.'

Throughout the summer the valley, beautifully sheltered, blossomed with plants that were difficult to raise anywhere else in Shetland. The garden rampaged with a riotous mixture of weeds and shrubs and Sister Mary Aidan found among them a small natural bower where she kept the grass trimmed and where she sometimes sat. The place, hung about by draping foliage, had curtained itself so as to reveal a gap, a window through which one could look out upon a haunting vista. Indeed, from this spot one could commune with beauty, with the green undulating roll of the land and the purple hills spliced by the ocean, standing like sentinels, a seaway into the valley.

I too had enjoyed this leafy shelter of privacy and peace on the rare occasion I had sat there. To drink in such solitude, filled with the sounds of the countryside and with the quiet company of Barnabas, was a delight. Barney, who was not a little lazy, liked to lie sun-baked nearby. While Pippin, petite and entirely opposite in nature, could only tease. Life was all hunting or play for her.

Today we had felt the first nips of autumn, the season that was so scant it was hardly a season at all and that had, before one realized it, allowed winter to bite into the bones. The deluge of the past 24 hours had seeped through the dry timbers and felt roof of Da Gaets and Sister now turned her thoughts once more towards months of battling with the elements, electricity cuts, darkness, cold and damp.

'Life is full of ifs,' I said, 'isn't it? If only the house was ours and if only we had sufficient money to insulate and renovate it, just imagine how such improvements would change things, would make the whole house feel warmer and lighter and give you that extra space for those visitors of yours needing times of quietness.'

Several friends on the Westside had visited Sister. Some had stayed for an hour or so of 'quietness', and desired to stay longer. However, the house did not adapt itself easily to this type of ministry, especially in the darker periods of the year.

'Look, let's plan what we'd do if we had the money,' I suggested. 'Let's start the ball rolling in the direction we think it should go . . . So often, I think that our Lord must like to see us making a start on things, don't you? Sort of showing some initiative before he steps in.'

So we began dreaming about the things we would do if only we had the money; of how we could change the house, make the chapel just a little larger, twist the stairs around and have a toilet upstairs. What 'fun' it was, redesigning the place, putting in larger windows to let in more light, making a little track to bring the car to the door. Goodness, we were almost living in it by the time we stopped to say Compline.

'It would be nice,' Sister said, as we continued the conversation the next morning before I left to return to Fetlar, 'but it's not likely to happen though, is it? It's a pipe dream because we haven't any money and we aren't likely to have any.' She laughed teasingly, 'I'll simply have to go on being a martyr . . .'

On Fetlar a week or so later, in the midst of our busy visitors' season, we had an unexpected lull. 'Look, now that we've got a couple of days with no guests,' I said to everyone after Vespers, 'let's make the most of it and enjoy having space.' Cheerily, we went off to our various corners, but a couple of hours later, Sybil's telephone rang:

'Hello, Sybil,' said Janet Kelly, one of our island friends, 'I've been trying to get hold of one of you. You see, I've a couple of people needing accommodation . . .'!

Sybil tracked me down as I was having my supper and explained that Janet and her husband Peter, who were renovating their guesthouse, hoped that we could help them with a visitor problem. 'Apparently,' she went on, 'a "nice couple", a retired doctor and his wife, have arrived on Fetlar, desperate for somewhere to spend the night. And since the last ferry's gone, Mother, they can't get back to civilization on Yell. Well, Janet wonders . . . could we have them? She did say that there's no other accommodation available on the island this week, and if she took them in they'd literally have to sleep on the floor. She just thought that we might have an empty unit.'

'We'll have to say yes . . . oh blow,' I murmured under my breath, 'when we'd had such happy thoughts about throwing our feet in the air. I'll ask Sister Mary Clare to give us a hand . . . and if you could say to Janet, yes, all right, send them over. Thank you, Sybil . . . presumably they've got a car?'

Half an hour later, having scuttled around, made the beds, vacuumed the unit and arranged a pot of flowers, we greeted the couple. 'Welcome, welcome,' I said.

As I have said before, life is providential. Our two guests, Paul and Fay, a delightful couple, extended their stay beyond the one night and were with us for a week. On the evening before they left, they had coffee with me in the upstairs sitting room. 'What a gorgeous window you've got,' Fay said, sitting in front of it. 'Yes,' said Paul, 'it's a nice view too, but do tell us, because we're intrigued, who's this sister you've been speaking of who lives . . . did you say on the Shetland Mainland?'

I told them briefly of what a spiritual presence Sister was becoming on the Westside and then a little more about her situation living out in the Culswick valley. Showing surprising interest, Paul asked how possible it would be for us to find her other accommodation, 'something that's a little more suitable and nearer to the mainland bus route. And if you'll excuse me asking,' he said, 'would you be in a position to buy a property?' I had laughed merrily, explaining that we had about £150 in the bank.

Paul's eyes glistened and he leaned forward and began telling me about a London-based charitable trust that he knew. 'Look,' he said, 'why not put some sort of presentation together stating your needs and see if they can help. And don't go asking for a measly few thousand. Ask for something sensible towards, say, building a house. Actually, come to think of it, it would make better sense if first of all you acquired a piece of land upon which to build. Bear in mind, though, that if you do go ahead, you'll be dealing with a collection of hard-headed businessmen who'll want all the answers and facts.' He smiled. 'Actually, though, having said that, underneath the hard-headed side of things, I think you'll find a lot of kindness and good will.'

Despite having no money we stepped into the unknown, finding to our surprise that there were various possibilities of land. At first, we trailed around a complexity of openings, and this in a providential way led us to the door of some

Methodist friends. These lovely people gave us good advice, with one of the ministers even suggesting that we consider buying an old property that belonged to them. Sadly this house would have needed a lot of work and money spent on it – and it was lined with asbestos. Nevertheless, that same week, Colin, another minister of their group and a close friend of Sister Mary Aidan's, told her that there was a rectangular-shaped bungalow that was much more suitable for us standing on the top of a hill at the 'Brig a Waas', also on the Westside.

'It's owned by a man called Matty Johnson,' Sister told me excitedly over the telephone. 'Colin suggested that we ring him soon and ask for more information. Mother, you're going to be very cross, but I found Matty's number straightaway . . . and well, I spoke to his partner, Pat. It was staggering really, because she asked if I'd like to go over and have coffee with her. In fact, Mother, well, I've already been! She came and picked me up. She's very nice, and the house is just perfect for us, and she said they'd leave all the furnishings, carpets and everything . . .'

I couldn't stem the enthusiasm that surged down the phone into my ear as she described the location, the views, each room and every piece of furniture. 'Oh, you'll just love it, Mother, and there's a nice area around it, which could be a lovely garden, and it's only a 20-minute walk from the bus stop and I could easily manage that . . .'

'Stop!' I yelled. 'It's not ours yet, and anyway, why do they want to sell it?'

'They want to emigrate to New Zealand, soon, and so would like to get it sold. Pat said that I'm to bring you to tea next time you're over so that you can see it and we can discuss things. Oh yes, and interestingly, it's exactly the price that Paul's suggesting that we ask from the charity.'

Visiting Pat and Matty the next time that I was on the Westside, I found that I too liked them a lot. I had a strange feeling that one day the house would be ours. The couple were equally convinced that we were meant to purchase the property, despite the fact that we had no money and they wanted a quick sale.

Immediately, for now there was little time before Rosemary and I set off for Medjugorje, I set to work on a presentation to the charitable trust that Paul had recommended. Stating our needs as simply and straightforwardly as I could, I posted the document to him for his perusal, to pass on to the charity's administrator.

On the day Paul received my package I arrived home from a trip to Lerwick to find the telephone ringing. A male voice asked if he could speak to Mother Mary Agnes.

'This is Mother,' I said.

'Oh good, this is Paul, Mother. I thought I would let you know that your presentation arrived this morning. Actually, I'm so impressed with it that I'd like to ask you a few questions – business questions.'

My heart sank, for being something of a businessman himself I guessed that he would fire some crackers. He did, but fortunately, having done our homework with regard to the sale, I knew the answers.

'Well,' he announced, 'since you're such an astute young lady . . .'

Goodness, I thought, I'm neither astute nor young . . .

'. . . Since you're such an astute young lady, and since you've given me the right sort of answers, I'm pleased to say that I'd like to buy the property for you myself.'

Totally pole-axed, I sank into the chair behind me, unable to speak while Paul continued: 'There are, of course, certain conditions, three of them.' He told me exactly what they

Redshank

were. All of them we were happily able to take on board and subsequently our instructions for the buying of St Mahri's Hame were put into the hands of our solicitor.

God leads us where he will and in such amazing and often surprising ways. Almost immediately after this incredible incident Rosemary and I set off on another such journey in Christ – to Medjugorje.

We had arranged to sail from Lerwick to Aberdeen and then travel to London by train, where we would meet the rest of the party with whom we were to fly to Croatia. Setting off from Shetland at 6 p.m., we watched the little houses on the quayside slide away from us as we stood by our cabin window. A rainbow illuminated the western sky, dispelling a little of our yearning for home into joy. Deep inside I somehow knew that this journey was significant and that heaven was wishing us Godspeed.

The next morning, peering from the top bunk I saw, in a bleary-eyed sort of way, that Rosemary was already up, dressed and looking horribly awake. 'Hello,' I murmured, 'did you have a good night?'

She turned and looked up, elated. 'Mother, I must tell you

something. I had a dream last night . . .' Her announcement surprised me into immediate attentiveness, for Rosemary, who always had her feet so firmly placed on the ground was, as we know, not given to sentimentality or dreaming. 'You see,' she went on, 'Our Lady came to me.' The statement was bold and without trimming. 'And I feel a whole lot better now about going.'

Easing myself on to an elbow, I rubbed my eyes.

After my friend's initial enthusiasm about going to Medjugorje, I realized that she had become increasingly worried that she wasn't going to enjoy any of, what she called, 'the floweriness' of it all. When I had questioned her, her reply was, 'Oh you know, lots of people walking around saying the rosary all the time.' What I did know was that Rosemary herself had carried a rosary in her pocket for the past 20 years and used it regularly, both in our community recitation of the devotion and privately. It was simply with regard to custom and culture that Rosemary, like most Anglicans, did not readily wear her soul on her sleeve.

'Tell me more,' I encouraged, leaning out of bed.

'Our Lady,' she said, 'came to me . . . and she told me that I should try to accept that there were many different ways of worshipping her Son and that I was to try and be more tolerant and, well, happy for people with different views . . . That was all, really. Anyway, I feel a whole lot better about it now and don't think that I'll mind so much.'

On our first morning in Medjugorje it was suggested that our party walk across the fields to the old village, to 'Vicka's house'. There we would, with any luck, see Vicka herself. She was, as we knew, one of the six visionaries and was scheduled to talk to a group of pilgrims after breakfast. We arrived to find about a hundred people gathered in the sunshine around her home.

The house, with a tile or two off the roof, stood perched on the lower slopes of the hillside upon which Our Lady had first appeared to the children. We mingled with the crowd, an international mix of pilgrims, who overflowed from an approximately 20-foot by 20-foot vine-covered courtyard, surrounded by a wall and stepped down from the building. A congestion of folk had already squashed under the shade of the foliage with their cameras loaded, hoping to get a picture of the girl as she came down from the house. We latecomers, with little hope of seeing much, splayed out in gaggles across a dusty road full of bucket-sized potholes where hens pecked nervously along its fringes. The shoulder-height wall was draped with swinging legs and this looked a good place from which to view, if a little perilous. Amid a buzz of optimistic chatter, studded with bursts of Hail Marys or a hymn to Our Lady, there was a great air of festivity.

After 20 minutes or so, a moment of silence brushed the air, in prelude to an almighty roar. I looked up in the direction that everyone else seemed to be peering and saw that there were shadowy movements behind a glass-fronted veranda around part of the house. Then a door opened and a young woman of average height, a little on the plump side, wearing simple, casual-looking clothing which included a very English sort of cardigan, came out. She ran down a flight of steps that dropped through the vines and then for a moment disappeared from view. As neatly as possible I wove my way through a wave of people until, thoroughly wedged among bodies, I squinted through a cluster of leaves.

My first impression of the young woman was that her whole being glowed. Totally empty of self, in the kind of way that should be natural to all of us, she was radiating heaven to every eye riveted upon her. Quietness descended over the scene and she greeted us in her own language and then quietly waited for her words to be translated by her four interpreters. Questions were asked and each answer carefully relayed. Caught rigidly and rather uncomfortably among a company of French ladies, I managed to glance around – my head being about the only part of me I could move. I wondered where Rosemary and the rest of our party were, and hoped that they could see.

Vicka continued to speak and I was increasingly awed by the knowledge of what I beheld. Here was a woman in her early thirties who was not giving an audience to a group of people in order to present herself, but who was, through her total abandonment to God, sharing heaven with a crowd of yearning people. She was showing forth Christ, physically, mentally and with all her soul. She, in her peacefulness, simplicity and joy, was a perfect channel of the great King. She was, as we all should be, an instrument of love.

In contradiction of this, and just to remind me afresh that the world is also a place of discord, a woman jostled herself in front of me, physically elbowing me out of the way. My hip and left leg were painful anyway and now I was so tightly imprisoned among bodies that there was not even space to manoeuvre myself on to my seat-stick.

Anxious that Rosemary was also having her toes trodden on, I craned my head again and caught an unexpected glimpse. Doing a double take I looked again. Astonishingly, quite astonishingly, and how I have no idea, she was perched high on the wall and looking as pleased as punch! 'Please God, don't let her fall . . .' Praying thus I jerked my nose out of someone's ponytail now bobbing in front of me.

Between people's heads, ribbons and hairstyles, and through the leaves, I peered again at Vicka. She looked directly at me, and smiled. Her smile seemed uniquely for me, though later I laughed at my arrogance, for of course she was sharing her

God with the world . . . nevertheless, her glance remains with me still.

Later, with something of a struggle, I helped Rosemary from the wall and we joined the rest of our group. Thankfully, Father Rodney suggested that we have a cup of coffee at the nearby café, located immediately around the corner where the track began its ascent up the Hill of the Apparitions. We heaved ourselves up a short gradient and then a few steps higher to a vine-covered patio spread about with tables and there, thankfully, we sat down.

As we sipped our hot drink and gazed towards the range of distant mountains, our companions' talk turned to the strange phenomenon of people's 'rosaries turning gold'.

'Yes,' said Father Rodney, 'some people who come here, have found with great astonishment that the metal links of their rosary have turned gold! It seems to happen randomly and without rhyme or reason.' Looking across the table I saw a shadow of aggravation flit across Rosemary's face. She looked down and I knew that she was avoiding any participation in the conversation.

'It happened to me, you know,' Father Rodney said, glancing at Rosemary. 'It was after our first visit here and we were on our way home on the coach. I took my rosary out of my pocket and all the links had turned gold.'

'Yes, it happened to me too,' said another lady in our party, pulling her rosary from her pocket and embarking on her own tale.

Concerned that my friend might, as was her Yorkshire wont, bring everyone to earth with a bump, I somewhat nervously continued to observe her. Without at all realizing that she had done so, she pulled her own very ordinary rosary out of her pocket and held it in her hands.

'Yes, it's most extraordinary,' said Father. Rosemary frowned across at me and I remembered the discussion we had had on the ship a few days earlier when she had declared that all this 'rosary business' was probably a gimmicky thing. 'You know, something to do with the way that the rosaries are made.'

Interestingly, I later read the following in a book: 'Vicka says that the Blessed Mother smiled when she saw the delight of so many pilgrims whose rosaries turned gold during the recitation of the rosary on a cold winter evening of her apparition in mid-January 1982. Vicka says that the Blessed Mother told her that golden rosaries are meant to be a sign that prayer changes human hearts, human circumstances, human endeavours: "Prayer changes all life on earth and hereafter".'[1]

Coffee almost over, Father Rodney asked if we were ready for our pilgrimage up the hill. 'It's steep in places and slippery, so be very careful,' he said, casting a meaningful glance at us. Rosemary swallowed the last of her coffee, placed her cup on the table and glanced down at her other hand, slightly wondering why she was holding her rosary. For the rest of my life I shall remember her look of utter incredulity, and her loud exclamation: 'It's turned gold!'

A day or two later I said how wonderful I thought the happening had been. She considered me for a moment or two and then replied in her gruff manner, which I am sure caused Our Lady, as well as Our Lord, much mirth: 'Well . . . I really rather liked it as it was!'

In an incredibly warm and homely way, Our Lady always seems near. Indeed, I have felt greatly comforted by the thought of her presence through this wild night and remember so well the time in Medjugorje when I first recognized her 'in truth'.

The parish church of St James in Medjugorje was crammed with pilgrims, standing, sitting or kneeling. Rosemary and I, thor-

oughly squashed into a pew, were caught up in a great babble of sound, the sound of hundreds of voices reciting the rosary in different languages. It was hot and my hip was painful; added to that, the air was heavy with the odour of perspiring bodies. We had been there for over an hour and had been led in the saying of the joyful and then the sorrowful mysteries. Now we were moving into the first glorious mystery of our Lord Jesus Christ . . .

Unexpectedly, in fact almost violently, I felt anguish such as I had never felt before and realized with utter surprise that warm tears were falling down my face. The anguish persisted and I wondered how on earth I could possibly be weeping when meditating upon so glorious a mystery as our Lord's resurrection? The answer came quickly and I knew that my sorrow was because Christ had been lifted up . . . into a glory beyond reach. His resurrection changed, separated and divided him from us, leaving us here, down among this noise, clamour, sweat and the heaviness of being human. Then – time spun, whirling the whole situation back to an instance from my childhood. Not the one when Mam had come to me in the night, but earlier; an instance that I had completely forgotten. This time I was a toddler and Mam and I were in a large store in Nottingham. She had let go of my hand, probably to pay for a purchase. I had stepped away and suddenly she had gone. Desperately I flung around through a forest of legs. Yes, the occasion felt exactly like now. Panicking, tears streamed down my face and I wanted my mother. I wanted to be found and lifted up and hugged. I wanted to be safe with the person I loved. Of course, she quickly found me . . . for I had never been lost. She snatched me to her and at that moment the childhood scene disappeared as quickly as it had come and I was conscious again of Medjugorje, and yet also of something else. Peace was being poured through the top of my head as though from a jug and it streamed into my being. The arms and legs and noise of people were still there around me, pushing and jostling, though they were different now, for life was different and nothing could ever disturb that which had been given. Now, whatever happened would be grounded in him, in Love, our God and in the glory of his resurrection, a resurrection that binds rather than separates. Now I was truly whole and fear could never again do more than scratch the surface of my life.

My fingers had continued to move along the rosary beads and I realized that only a few seconds had passed. Nevertheless, they were a few seconds, on that birthday of mine – the Church's old, discarded feast of the Motherhood of Our Lady – that had added a deep and lasting dimension of love to my life. No better birthday gift could have been given me – the gift of Mary's son in a new, intimate and eternal way.

13

Streams of Worship

We turned the key in the lock of the door of Da Gaets for the last time and groped up the path from its back entrance. We were both worn out, grimy, more than a bit fractious, and for me there was an underlying feeling of sadness. Da Gaets was austere, I had always known that, and yet it had helped mould SOLI. Yes, I mused, waving my torch in front of me, some of our deepest spiritual inspirations have grown out of this place and it hurts to say goodbye. We threw the last few bundles into the car and clambered inside ourselves. Switching on the headlights I splashed light over the great bulk of the removal van in front of us where two men were struggling to clamp down its back-end. Ten minutes later it lumbered into the night, winding before us into a new chapter of life. Significantly, today was the thirteenth anniversary of my having left Devon. It was the feast of Our Lady Immaculate . . . the feast of light and purity and love.

Sister Mary Aidan and I travelled the five or six miles between Da Gaets and St Mahri's Hame in weary silence, gearing ourselves up for the final effort of the day, helping to unload at the other end. Boxes and more boxes . . .

An hour or so later, by then completely dishevelled, we waved off the men. At last, shutting the door, we let the cats out of their carrying boxes and managed to make up a couple of beds in odd corners among the chaos. Pippin excitedly explored every nook and cranny for the rest of the night, while Barney found an armchair in which had been slung an appealing blanket. Sister Mary Aidan and her cats had arrived.

Several days after the move to St Mahri's Hame, I returned to Fetlar. Alison Jackson, now settled into the visitor's half of Weatherhead, was a month into her aspirancy. She was a quiet, reliable young woman with a cheery laugh and, I suspected, a deeply contemplative vocation. However, there was for her as there had been for all of us the process of coming to terms, not only with the aspects of the life but also with oneself. The coming to terms with the actual route along which God has asked one to walk is secondary. So she was at the beginning of a journey that is sometimes an incongruous process of learning to be faithful to God, to oneself and to others, in the smallest and the simplest of obediences. Predictably, that following Christmas our aspirant had a healthy attack of doubts regarding her possible SOLI vocation. Yet we should never mind these kinds of uncertainties, for they toughen and temper. Certainly for Alison, towards the end of her first couple of months with us, they were well timed to help her reflect upon her call at a different, deeper level.

By the spring, when the snows had cleared and the oyster-catchers were arriving, three of us had also arrived at a new burgeoning forward in our life in God. Sister Mary Aidan was now to make her Life Vows, I was to be ordained to the priesthood and Alison to be received as a postulant.

Alison knelt in front of the altar in the chapel of Christ the Encompasser, to be received and embraced into her new spiritual family of SOLI. Looking down on her in her youthfulness I moved into the next part of the service.

'Alison, will you, by the help of the Holy Spirit, adhere to the teachings of Christ's Holy Gospel?'

'I will.'

'Therefore, Alison, I ask you, do you desire to love and serve God, as a postulant within this family of SOLI, testing your vocation to the wholeness of a life in Christ, and living humbly and at peace in this place?'

'I do.'

Sister Mary Aidan's Life Profession took place in the church of St Magnus in Lerwick on the Shetland Mainland, for this location made it easier for our Shetland friends and for Sister's neighbours to attend. The church resounded with music as Frances played the organ. Later during the service Bishop Bruce received Sister's vows, placing the gold ring on her finger as the token of her life commitment to Christ, and then with a candle gave her her dedication:

'Do you, Sister Mary Aidan, of the Society of Our Lady of the Isles . . . offer and bind yourself to Almighty God, to live perpetually in his love . . .'

Firmly and surely she responded,

> 'With the aiding of the Father,
> the aiding of the Son,
> and the aiding of the Holy Spirit,
> I do.'

The Bishop bent, placed his hands upon her head and said:

> 'My daughter, I receive your Solemn Vows, and now
> dedicate you as Sister Mary Aidan of Our Lady of Light.'

My ordination took place two days after Sister Mary Aidan's profession and was another day to remember. This too was located away from Fetlar, in a tiny church, the most northerly in Britain's Anglican Communion, on the island of Yell. It was dedicated to another Celtic saint, St Colman, and like our service in St Magnus was full of loving friends not only from Shetland but also from much further afield.

All exterior things fell away as the ceremonial part of the service began and Sister Mary Clare and Father Lewis presented me to the Bishop. It was simple and focused entirely upon God. Still I can feel the anointing with oil in the palm of my right hand, the weight of the hands of our priestly friends on my head and the Bishop's words, 'Pour now upon her your Spirit . . .'

After these landmarks of blessing we were quickly grounded into the daily rhythm of our lifestyle and the steady flow of summer visitors. Sybil at this time was preparing to fly down to Aberdeen for major surgery and Rosemary was to join her.

Rosemary herself was causing us some anxiety health-wise due to the continuance of her chesty cough, which she dismissed as 'nothing', despite the fact that it was now hanging on into the summer.

'Are you sure that you're okay to go down to Aberdeen, Rosemary?' I asked her.

'Well, I do feel as though there's a bit of weight, something here,' she had said to me, placing a hand across her chest, 'and I get very out of breath. I can't seem to shake it off. I don't know what it is really. Anyway, I'm all right when I'm not doing anything too energetic.'

A week or so later Sister Mary Clare, fastening her safety-belt, switched on the car ignition and wound up the window while a reluctant Sybil, who hates leaving home at any time, leaned forward to call out her farewells. 'Really, I don't like going off and leaving you with Skerry so unwell, Mother,' she said. Of course, Sybil, who mostly feeds and cares for the cats, is totally twisted around Skerry's little paw!

'Don't worry, Sybil,' I called out. 'Skerry and I have an understanding about all sorts of things. Just take care of yourself.'

Skerry, not long before he died

'Bye-bye, Sybil,' called Rosemary. 'I'll see you at the end of the week.' Rosemary was travelling down later. The car wound its way up the Ness road and we waved it out of sight.

As always, Rosemary had been reluctant to go to the doctor and was just as determined as ever to join up with Sybil, whose operation was a great success, in Aberdeen. En route for home, the two of them stayed overnight at a guesthouse where they shared a room and it was then that Sybil became aware of just how ill Rosemary was.

'She coughed all night,' Sybil confided to me when they arrived home.

The past two winters Rosemary had been given antibiotics but now with each succeeding year we were aware that this 'winter chestiness' was becoming more and more difficult to throw off. 'I do wish the doctor would send you for an X-ray, Rosemary,' I said, for the umpteenth time and again she shrugged.

Skerry was also causing concern, but like most little

animals, especially those that know they are loved, he was heartbreakingly 'acquiescent'. My own acceptance of having soon to bid him farewell was not so easy, for he, with his brother Flugga, had been the dearest of companions to me each in their different ways from the time of my arrival on Fetlar. They had also been the first beloved members of my SOLI family and I knew that I, especially, would miss this unique little character.

We joke that we only have two seasons in Shetland – winter and July – and during this particular year even July was replaced by cold, wet days. How sorry we felt for our visitors who we were sure had no comprehension of how heavenly a Shetland summer can be. The days moved into August and the first week darkened into even deeper gloom, particularly for me, for our dear Skerry, at the age of 14, died at the vet's while having an operation. He had been ill and having treatment for several months for a rare condition which sadly affects older felines.

It is said that animals have no power of reasoning and therefore do not possess souls; however, having had such a loving friend as Skerry, I would argue endlessly with any theologian that the Church has ever had over this question. For I believe that every creature that is capable of loving has a soul. One has only to look into their eyes to know that they were created by love and for love. Similarly, I am persuaded that since love never dies neither do they. Daily we see the Spirit of God, the Spirit of Love, shining through the whole of his creation around us, be it grey or sunny. God is in all things, therefore his love is in all things, for God is Love and love, being eternal, cannot die.

When thinking of Skerry, I am more than convinced that he could not have been created by anyone other than God, for during his little life he showed this uniqueness in such characterful and dear ways. Certainly, and with all due respect to those who say otherwise about animals, he was able to reason and even to tease. He would go to the most enormous lengths to gain attention or the tiniest extra titbit, or anything else that he wanted. Even in his illness he could not help ribbing us. To me he was the most loyal and loving friend and no words will ever express how much I miss him – his feel, his look, his love and especially the bump of him on the end of my bed. Yet, as with any bereavement it is only for a while, for with him as with all whom we have loved and who we continue to love, he has gone home in exactly the same way that we shall all, one day, go home. This truth only leaves one to give thanks for the gift of our furry friends during our lifespan here and for the continuance of love's unbroken bond in heaven.

Aros, Sister Mary Clare's beautiful elderly puss, died within a couple of days of Skerry, and they were both buried in our new garden at Lark's Hame, with Tildy.

Yes, truly it was an autumn of departures, for the following month there was another. Sister Mary Clare left Fetlar for Orkney where we had seconded her for a year to help and work with Sybil Roebuck on Rousay.

My long night of the hurricane was almost over and it had been good, for all things, however terrible they might be, do, as St Paul tells us, work together for good to them that love. To them that love God in the essence of Truth is what I mean, rather than in merely human terms, human speculation or in the struggling of human knowledge. For to truly love is to merge with and become love, a love that shines.

Our merging with love, that is our abiding in Christ, should become as natural as breathing and, indeed, should become the very breath of life itself. And for us, for SOLI, this union with him is nourished by such things as solitude and worship. A lady who came to visit recently said that she had found, in the solitude and worship she had experienced here, a nurturing that gave her a growing sense of God's purpose in her daily lay person's life; 'my experience was transforming', she wrote.

This union with Christ is SOLI's vocation, a vocation in which God asks us to abide in him. It is a vocation in which we are asked to give ourselves to him in silence and in praise that he might use us as channels, and for us there is no better place to do this than in our small circular chapel. Christ himself is there, beautiful, simple, human, divine, utterly approachable and allowing us to be united with him. Sometimes his presence is so palpable that one can almost see and touch him. People shed tears – we do ourselves sometimes – for in the giving and the receiving worship becomes love and like Moses standing before the burning bush, metaphorically we take off our shoes. Yes, this place of communion with God is holy ground; it is the meeting place of love.

The window rocketed ajar again, yet despite the hassle a still small voice spoke through the storm:

'Worship is love, give worship . . .'

14

Freedom's Song

It was never easy trying to get Rosemary to go and see a doctor but after she returned home from the last holiday that she was ever to have, one that had been fraught with breathlessness, she succumbed. A new husband-and-wife medical team had taken on the practice on Yell, and after Rosemary's trip over to see them she was sent off to Lerwick for an X-ray. We were expecting the usual wait for the results, but they were returned at once. Rosemary was notified that she was being sent to the hospital in Aberdeen for more tests. So in a twinkling Rosemary and I found ourselves preparing for the trip, having been told that her symptoms could mean cancer. We waved goodbye to the family at home, not expecting to be away for more than a week.

Our friend Ann, who has a flat only a ten-minute walk away from the Aberdeen Royal Infirmary, met us at the airport and took us to her home. The following morning Rosemary was admitted to the hospital and from that moment her condition deteriorated. I spent hours sitting by her bedside or familiarizing myself with miles of hospital corridors. Days became weeks, my back became more painful and I walked nowhere without taking my Medjugorje seat-stick. Ann was a wonderful hostess who insisted that I stay with her for as long as I needed, and she often ran me back and forth in her car.

One morning, while I was sitting at Rosemary's bedside, a

young nurse asked if we would accompany her to a side-room off the ward. The room was bleak, with little more than two chairs placed haphazardly in the centre. Rosemary looked doleful and putting an arm around her shoulders I gave her a hug. She looked up and smiled. 'I just feel a little nervous,' she said.

There was the sound of footsteps, a few murmured words and the door swung inwards. A lean, rather efficient, white-coated gentleman stepped towards us, accompanied by the same young nurse. Hastily vacating my chair I pushed it towards him. With a quick gesture of his hand he declined the offer to sit and wasting little time on preliminaries, spoke of the final results of Rosemary's tests.

' You have adenocarcinoma – a type of cancer of the lungs . . .'

Rosemary said nothing and I knew that she had 'disen-gaged' herself. Her eyes were unseeing and her whole being seemed switched into a state of heavy gloom. There were no questions that she wanted to ask, yet the consultant was making it abundantly clear, to me at any rate, that our friend had limited time.

Prompting her to ask a couple of necessary questions with regard to her condition, I became increasingly aware that she had not the slightest interest. The doctor smiled wanly and again saying that he was sorry suggested that we might like to sit in the wee room a while longer.

'Yes, let's stay here,' Rosemary grunted, putting a re-straining hand on my arm and showing the first hint of communication. The door shut and she looked across at me. 'I hope I'll get to Joan and David's golden wedding in the spring. They're expecting me, you know . . . I'll ask the doctor about it the next time I see him.'

From what the doctor had said, I knew there was no

chance that Rosemary would ever travel to Yorkshire again. However, she was now keen to talk and clasped my arm. 'We'll have to make the most of every moment left to us . . .'

'And we will,' I replied.

Later that day, while she was sleeping, I crept away to get myself a mug of coffee and to meet up with Sylvia, our hospital chaplain friend and Caim member. Sylvia in turn introduced me to a nurse friend of hers who worked on one of the cancer wards, who gave me a much clearer picture with regard to the illness. She reassured me that our island nurse would be qualified to give all the help needed and that any necessary equipment would be provided.

That evening, looking at Rosemary propped up against a mound of pillows, I realized afresh how frail my robust friend had become. She opened her eyes and searching her face again I sought to understand how things were with her. At that moment Ann crept into the ward to collect me. After a while I stood, gave Rosemary a hug and then placed my hands gently on her head:

'The encircling of your friends and loved ones, be upon you,
the encircling of the saints be upon you,
the encircling of the angels be upon you
and the blessing of the Father of us all be upon you
this night and for ever.'

Rosemary was one of the largest-hearted people I have ever known and I had always been aware of her deep affection for me, but in her gruff way she never actually showed much emotion of loving, and certainly never any of 'that surface stuff'. That night, as I limped away from her bed, she was staring down at her hands that lay, now fragile-looking, against the sheet. With great boldness, as I left I told her that we loved her. Turning again a moment or two later for a final wave, I saw tears streaming down her face. 'I love you too,' she mouthed.

The days passed. Rosemary's sister Joan arrived to spend a few days in Aberdeen with us, streams of friends from far and near visited, including Bishop Bruce, clergy from the diocese and some of our own Caim members.

During our days of coming to terms with the prognosis, one of the team of doctors came to talk with Rosemary and she asked him precisely how long her life expectancy was and whether, in fact, she would make it to the much anticipated golden wedding celebration. 'When is it?' he enquired.

'In seven months' time,' she answered.

'You'll be lucky,' was his blunt reply.

Eventually Rosemary was moved upstairs to a cancer ward to begin her chemotherapy treatment. Here at the top of the hospital, to my delight she was able to accept her situation and suddenly took on a new lease of life. She shared a small room with only three other people, including a child, and the place was homely and cheerful with its windows thrown open to the skies and even a longed-for fan on her bedside table. The staff members were wonderful, for nothing was ever too much trouble for them. I could visit when I wished and never felt in the way. Rosemary beamed at me each time I walked into her new quarters and she remarked on how wonderful it was to have a view of the sea, albeit a distant one. I agreed, for to us it was sustenance to the soul, so starved were we of our sea-surrounded home.

During her stay in hospital Rosemary doggedly wrote her last will and testament and we discussed her wishes with regard to her funeral. A helpful Macmillan nurse came to chat with us and by the time she was allowed to return to Shetland Rosemary was her cheery self and full of laughter.

We were not expecting the journey home to be easy and we were right, for things in the far north are rarely as simple as they sound. Having located a wheelchair for Rosemary after the ambulance had dropped us at the airport, I then dealt with getting our luggage checked in – happily without hitch. After that, we sat watching the bustle of the busy terminal as the world flashed by, first for one hour and then for two. To start with it was fun, though after three and then four hours of waiting for the fog to lift sufficiently for our flight to be called I was anxious. Rosemary was getting tired, weary enough to jump me into leaving her awhile. I went off to make some enquiries.

Walking through a swirl of people by the check-in desks I was brought up short by an announcement over the intercom, 'Will all passengers for Shetland please report to the BA desk to be given further information.' A scrum of bodies bundled past me and before I knew it I was standing somewhere at the end of a queue. Long before reaching the source of information I discovered that all the Shetland-bound passengers were being bussed to the docks. The ship was due to sail in an hour!

When I reached the harassed person behind the desk, she took my details and snapped two P&O meal vouchers into my hand, saying that the coach was waiting and would I, with my friend, board at once. I explained that my friend was in a wheelchair and that she was not capable of 'boarding' a bus. The lady reiterated that we needed to board the coach – now. I rarely speak sharply but my concern for Rosemary knew no bounds and I asked to see her boss. She disappeared, to return five minutes later with an official-looking man to whom I repeated our predicament and who instantly reinstated my faith in British Airways.

'If you could possibly call a taxi for us and ring P&O

Ferries to tell them that we're on the way and to have a wheelchair waiting, I'd be so grateful,' I trotted out, looking at my watch.

To my further relief, the gentleman conceded that he would do exactly that, and that I need have no more worries. 'At your expense?' I asked with a smile and he nodded and called a porter to assist us into the cab. Ten minutes later, with a determined driver at the wheel, we sped off in the direction of the docks. True to the 'boss's' word, all was accomplished smoothly, that is, apart from a rush-hour hold-up on the outskirts of the city. Nevertheless, the ship waited for us, along with three hefty stewards and a second wheelchair. To Rosemary's horror they physically carried the chair, with her in it, up the gangway into the boat – not her most pleasurable experience, though well worth it, we decided, once we were aboard. One of the men carried our cases to a cabin, which had every facility, including a large window by which we later sat and said Compline.

'Oh Mother, this is bliss, and so much more peaceful than going by air,' Rosemary twinkled, suddenly quite perky after her sleep in the taxi and remembering nothing about traffic hold-ups or the driver's panic that the ship might have sailed!

I collected our supper on a tray, and we sat and ate it by our window as the huge ferry cruised, like the queen that she was, behind the pilot boat and out of the harbour. Half an hour later we were drifting across the palest of liquid green seas, tinged with the melting pinks of sunset and softened and diffused in the evening haze. It was a calm crossing that night and the 14-hour voyage, peaceful. On the strength of it we decided that this was the way to travel on our future three-weekly trips to the hospital for treatment. Rosemary could take her time, sleep in a comfortable bed, and be fresh for the next day. Additionally, since the ship officially docked in Shetland at eight o'clock in the morning, it meant that we could get back to Fetlar on the same day.

It was an uneventful night and we both slept well, though having lived for nearly 15 years in Shetland, we were under no illusions about the ocean always being so obligingly quiescent. We knew that to choose to sail would be to risk storms, sometimes of huge proportions. In fact, the first one came later in the month on our very next journey. On that trip we were returning home and I had collected a supper tray from the ship's cafeteria. Again we had our meal by the window of our cabin and as always it was enjoyable eating it within the relative stillness of the port but goodness, when the ship sailed out of the harbour gates and hit the high seas, it was a different story. Instantly, we were rolled this way and that and up and down, like a boat in a tub, and knew beyond doubt that we must get into our bunks and lie flat.

Quickly, I helped Rosemary to settle and then concentrated on myself. In the toilet room I was bashed back and forth, into the washbasin and then into the shower fittings. Feeling sick, I decided that this was one night of my life that I was not going to wash. Rapidly I finished brushing my teeth and then opening the door back into the cabin allowed myself to be swung out by its handle. Righting myself I saw Rosemary out of the corner of my eye tucked up in bed. She has always been irritatingly strong about such things and was laughing.

'Get into bed quickly.'

'Don't worry, Rosemary. You might not believe it, but that's exactly where I'm aiming!'

Firstly, however, it was imperative to make sure that our supper tray was lodged on the table between us and I made checking it my last and only job before being hurled into my bunk. The table had an inch-high ridge around it so I thought that the tray would stay secure. Pulling the bedclothes over my head I hoped that all would be well. The night grew progressively dark and the storm boiled into a great cauldron of wrath. Waves slashed, buffeting the vessel so that every joint of its frame groaned and creaked, squeaked, squealed, screamed and every rivet and screw seemed to rattle. In my bunk I held on to the short bed-rail most of the night, sure that I would be tossed right out and over the top. Fortunately both Rosemary and I stayed put, though the supper tray was not so lucky and jumped over its ridge on to the floor. Fumbling around, I flashed my torch across the implements now slithering around and groaned. There was no other way; I needed to get out of bed and deal with it, if only to stop the din. Incredibly, Rosemary slept through my splendid show of gymnastics and, adding to my relief, I found that the ship's thick crockery had come to no harm.

The sea continued to roar like a frenzy of dragons, each battling for a chance to bat us this way and that, and certainly it took its toll of me before our ship moved into calmer waters. How relieved we were to glide, like an ice-maiden, into the lee of Shetland, into the still coolness of dawn, and to find a cheerful group of SOLI-ites waiting on the quayside. Sister Mary Clare, Sister Mary Aidan and Alison all helped us into the car, after which we drove to the nearest café for a really hot and calming drink.

It was only a short time after this that Alison's new name in religion was chosen for her. The ceremony took place in the chapel of Christ the Encompasser.

Standing in front of the large central window of the chapel I faced Alison, who was kneeling before the altar at a small prayer-desk. On the altar had been placed the basket in which, this time, there were only three names: Sister Mary Julian, after Mother Julian of Norwich, Sister Mary Brigid, after the great Celtic saint, Brigid of Ireland, and Sister Mary Cuthbert, after Cuthbert of Lindisfarne, friend of St Aidan.

We bent into the silence of prayer:

'O Lord our God, guide our hand in the choosing of
the name
by which your daughter, Alison, will be known in religion.
Grant also that having chosen her name this day, she may
continually grow in wisdom and in strength, and that,
with your blessing and aid,
she may ever please you in the glorifying of your, own,
most Holy Name.'

Pulling the folded slip from the basket I gave it to her. She opened it, crying out, 'It's the one I hoped it'd be, Mother – it's St Cuthbert. I'm going to be Sister Mary Cuthbert!'

Soon after this, Alison went into retreat in preparation for her great day, which was arranged for the Feast of St Raphael. The rest of us also prepared for the feast in a number of ways and looked forward to the arrival of guests coming for the occasion.

The Julian Room, which is our little sacristy, was full of sunshine. As I lifted the chasuble over my head I could hear the final strains of the organ prelude. The sound of hushed voices and the scrape of feet had stopped moving past the door and within the chapel itself the last few notes of sound had trembled into the silence of waiting. Our congregation in the chapel of Christ the Encompasser and of all his Holy Angels, waited. We all waited, and Alison waited, to be received this day as a novice of SOLI.

In the sacristy, I waited a moment or two more myself . . . standing alone and solitary as I have so often stood, yet in the presence of our Lord Jesus Christ, to whom I offered all that I was, stripping away all that was superfluous, proud or savouring of vainglory. Thus, empty of self, I prayed that Christ might be 'all' and I only the instrument of his love. Then, as ready as one can be and with the joyous feeling of lightness, I drew open the door. I moved into the doorway of the chapel. Everyone stood and I greeted them with the familiar words: 'Grace and peace to you from God our Father and the Lord Jesus Christ.'

Lark's Hame

The organ roared into the opening bars of the first hymn, 'Ye watchers and ye holy ones'. It was St Raphael's Day, a glorious one, and the chapel seemed full of angels as well as humans. Full of joyous anticipation and wonder we sang, 'Raise the glad strain, Alleluya! '

Walking over to my seat I glanced quickly around at my spiritual family. Sister Mary Clare, who was the cantor for the service, smiled; Sister Mary Aidan, who was server as well as preacher for that day, bowed slightly. The hymn went on, 'Thou bearer of the eternal Word . . .'

Alison looked composed and happy. In the congregation was her elder, ordained sister who had come to Fetlar for the occasion and would be taking her part in the service too. 'All saints, triumphant, raise the song . . .'

I gave thanks that Rosemary was with us for this important benchmark in SOLI's journey. Her eyes laughed across at me, knowingly. How was she able to sing like that, I had asked her. 'Oh, I can somehow sing over the top of my voice,' she explained.

> O friends, in gladness let us sing,
> Supernal anthems echoing,
>> Alleluya, Alleluya!
> To God the Father, God the Son,
> And God the Spirit, Three in One,
>> Alleluya, Alleluya, Alleluya, Alleluya, Alleluya![1]

The eucharistic service proceeded, incorporating the ceremony of the receiving of a novice – the declaration of intent, the blessing of the habit and the giving of the name in religion, the blessing of the cord, the blessing and the giving of a Celtic cross, the blessing and giving of a candle, and finally the blessing of the new Sister herself. Laying my hands upon her head I prayed the prayer that had been prayed over me when I had set out to found SOLI:

> 'Sister Mary Cuthbert,
> unto God's most gracious
> mercy and protection
> we commit you.
> May he keep you
> ever close to himself,
> that you may find

in his love
your strength and peace.
May he give you
the true courage
which shows itself
in gentleness;
the true wisdom
which shows itself
in simplicity;
the true power
which shows itself
by modesty.
May he guard you
from stumbling,
and set you
before the presence
of his glory
in exceeding joy.'

For a few moments it seemed as though the storm was abating and what a relief that was. Soon it would be time to get up, though there would be no streaks of dawn until long after rising. It had been a scary night and yet once again I rejoiced in the shielding of Christ. Almost a year ago, a new dawn had broken for Rosemary when she too had rested, enfolded in him. On the morning of her last day upon earth, it was obvious that she was on the brink of departure, and from eight o'clock that morning I sat quietly at her bedside. At one point, awaking from disturbed slumber, she smiled and summoned enough strength to beckon me closer. 'I want to say something,' she rasped. 'You – are – my – closest family . . .'

I knew that she loved her blood family deeply, though I also knew that spiritually this was a touching accolade of her trust and loyalty to me as a friend. What I did not know was that these were to be her last real words to me. After a while she indicated, now feebly, that her feet were cold. Quickly I refilled a hot-water bottle and placing it near her toes I also warmed them with my hands. They grew colder, until gradually all feeling slipped away, and she signalled me to return to my chair. Sitting down, I continued my watch while she snoozed, fitfully. Individuals slipped in and out of the room and Sybil brought me a tray laid with a bite of breakfast. Halfway through the morning Rosemary's eyes flickered again.

Bending towards her, I whispered, 'Would you like me to give you your communion?' She nodded, though immediately dropped into an uneasy sleep. Her breathing was now becoming laboured and I was relieved to have Fiona, our island nurse, call in to check her.

A couple more hours flicked past and silently I watched and waited until she felt strong enough to again open her eyes and nod her assent. Then, thankful beyond words for my priesthood, I administered to her the last rites and after receiving her communion she slept.

The window was slightly open, and this in itself was an amazing occurrence on Fetlar in January. I was further surprised to hear birdsong. The winter up here has its own often violent symphonies of sound, though for me they have never included such an outpouring as that which I now heard, that of a tiny lark bursting its lungs. Gently squeezing Rosemary's hand I asked if she too could hear the singing and she nodded. I knew that we were both remembering the same incident of years before and that Rosemary would be in no doubt as to the imminence of her journey. We had often talked together of birds being God's harbingers of heaven, the tiny heralds that welcome God's beloved ones home. Twenty years or so previously Rosemary herself had sat at the bedside of a dying Sister, Sister Margaret of Posbury, in Devonshire, who was to all appearances unconscious.

'I was sitting quietly with her,' Rosemary told me one day when we were sharing experiences of death, 'when suddenly the sound of a blackbird singing down in the woodland caught my attention. I asked Sister if she too could hear it and to my pleasure she squeezed my hand.'

In response to what she had said, I shared my own experience of birdsong at a similarly poignant moment, also at Posbury. This time it had been at the death of Mother Teresa, with whom Sister Margaret had co-founded the Order. On this occasion it had happened in the early hours of the morning, moments after she had passed away. Having returned to my cell I became instantly aware, as I stepped through its door, of the unforgettable strains of a nightingale. Never had I heard such song before nor ever have I since. Leaning on the narrow windowsill in the darkness I was transfixed by the melody of the lone bird, by its heartrending prelude wafting over the sleeping countryside and beckoning her forth.

Now, here in my room on Fetlar, as I got out of bed and lifted Flugga on to the floor, I thought how appropriate it was that a lark should sing for Rosemary. How appropriate it was that any bird should sing for her who was so great a naturalist. Fittingly, the title of my second autobiographical book telling of the growth of SOLI, in which Rosemary played so great a part, is called The Song of the Lark – or, in other words, in the context of the book itself, 'the Song of Love'.

Rosemary's own life was truly one of faithfulness in love, as was verified by the long list of close friends we had to notify of her death. There were friends from her childhood, her youth, her land army days, her two colleges, her teaching years, her work with the handicapped and the deaf, her years at Posbury, her years in Ilfracombe and last but not least her blissfully happy years in

Shetland. Yes, love was the keynote, as were song, rejoicing and laughter. Certainly she wanted her funeral to be a great celebration and especially asked that this Siegfried Sassoon poem should be read:

> *Everyone suddenly burst out singing;*
> *And I was filled with such delight*
> *As prisoned birds must find in freedom,*
> *Winging wildly across the white*
> *Orchards and dark fields; on − on − and out of sight.*
>
> *Everyone's voice was suddenly lifted;*
> *And beauty came like the setting sun:*
> *My heart was shaken with tears; and horror*
> *Drifted away . . . O, but Everyone*
> *Was a bird; and the song was wordless; the singing*
> *   will never be done.*[2]

15

Prelude to Eternity

Rosemary's own winging to God was ten minutes after midnight at the end of that long day of waiting. Those of us on Fetlar – Sister Mary Cuthbert, Sybil, Jean, Frances and Jane, a close island friend of Rosemary's – sat around her as she breathed her last and we were immediately caught up by a tangible feeling of joy, peace and fulfilment which so gloriously spilled over and into her funeral. The coffin sat in the centre of the chapel of Christ the Encompasser and there we had a 12-hour vigil of prayer throughout the night, each of us taking an hour at a time.

I had the great privilege of celebrating the Eucharist, at which Bishop Bruce, who flew up to Shetland at very short notice, preached. He began his sermon: 'If St John had been preaching here today he would have begun his sermon by saying, "In the beginning there was Sister Agnes and Rosemary...".' He went on to pay tribute to Rosemary and to say how it was she who had been SOLI's grounding. Indeed I heartily agreed, thanking God for Rosemary's good Yorkshire common sense and loyalty.

Islanders, Caim members, friends and relatives were with us for the service, as well as clergy from several denominations. The little chapel overflowed with those who loved her and with the sound of jubilance. Frances was our organist, drawing from us the triumphant praise that our friend had so relished.

At the end of our SOLI Eucharist, the coffin was carried out of chapel to the hearse and gently placed inside the vehicle. It was followed by a long cortège that wound its way west along the single-track road, across the island to the tiny church by the sea, situated on the edge of the beautiful crescent-shaped Tresta Bay. Here a second service was held. Rosemary's sister Joan read a lesson, Rosemary's friend Jane read a Celtic prayer, and I gave a homily to all who packed the building. Afterwards, Sister Mary Aidan, carrying the processional cross, led the Bishop, Father Lewis, the Revd Magnus Williamson, the minister of the Fetlar Kirk, and the Fetlar pallbearers, along with Rosemary's brother-in-law David, out of the Kirk with the coffin. The rest of us followed to the words of the Nunc Dimittis. At the graveside each member of SOLI said a short prayer. Magnus, with a voice that carried far over the waves, said the twenty-third psalm as the coffin was lowered into the grave and Father Lewis and I shared the words of the committal. After this, Bishop Bruce gave the final blessing before we each pulled off the red poppy that we were wearing and threw it into the grave. Sister Mary Clare had had the wonderful idea that since Rosemary had been born on 11 November, and had been called Rosemary for 'remembrance', and indeed was such a bright poppy-red sort of person that we should do this to honour her. About 200 poppies floated into the grave and we almost heard her laugh!

I gave thanks to God for the gift of my dear and most stalwart friend, Rosemary, a woman we all loved and will continue to love, for love is the one thing that we can be sure is imperishable. To a woman who loved God and through that love, loved us all. To Rosemary, a woman faithful in friendship and with the so rare quality these days of a deep Christian faith, grounded in prayer. To a woman with such a laugh that it ignited joy in the hearts of everyone. To Rosemary, who asked me to make her funeral, when it came, a day of great celebration. My heart paid tribute to a friend who gave me the gift of her trust, who trusted my call and shared it with me.

'May she rest in the love of God her dearest,
may she rest in the love of Christ his Son,
may she rest in the love of the Comforter Eternal,
ever rest in the Three in One.'

Epilogue

Another day had come, and around mid-morning sunlight spilled in through the windows of Lark's Hame. Truly out of darkness comes light and out of the tempest comes calm and with it today that reassurance of the closeness and glory of God.

Coming into my room to make my bed, I first removed a small friend who was now lying with his head on my pillow. Flugga is well used by now to being gathered up and moved and will obligingly curl wherever I put him. He settled into an armchair, hardly waking, and I returned to the other side of the room to pull back the sheets.

Christ, who gathers together the vastness of all that is and of all that revolves in space, Christ, who holds in himself the mystery of life, the very mystery of himself – he who is the gift of love, who is our warmth and light and singing. 'Oh, ro', as the Celts would say, a new day has dawned when the isles sing and when one knows that neither death nor any of life's storms can harm if we are truly centred in him.

Sitting on the edge of the bed, I bent to tighten a sandal. Over the years I have been swept constantly into fresh awareness of SOLI's vocation and now, in this place, with the hurricane over, I gave thanks for the uniqueness of what and who we are and are to become. Indeed, I gave thanks for the blessedness of the calling of every follower of Christ. And it is in and because of this blessedness that I can write no ending to my book, since there is no beginning nor end, to a tale in which its Epilogue is but the Prologue of another new chapter. No, I cannot write differently, for its Epilogue is the Prologue of God's continual calling of us into a deeper life. It is like a summer sunset in these isles that in a sudden blaze of glory merges with sunrise. So it is that our journeying on earth merges with our journeying in heaven, of which our minds, bodies and souls are but a part. Yes, they are but a part of a pulsating cycle, a spiral that at its optimum ascends upwards where Christ, risen and glorified, is the summit of our strivings.

Flugga

In half an hour I would celebrate the Eucharist. Standing, I made ready to go down to the chapel. Before leaving the room I paused and bent to stroke Flugga. He looked up and purred. Here, silently, in the eye of the storm, we are who we are, who God wants us to be and in that freedom we find wholeness.

Notes

Chapter 3 The Heavens Shake

1 'Poustinia' is a Russian word for a place of prayer.

Chapter 4 Thunderclouds Roll

1 'Caim' is a Celtic word meaning 'encompassment' or 'the circle around'. In the case of SOLI it is an extended group of friends who feel called to support us in a special way as part of our spiritual family.

Chapter 6 The Rhythm of Life

1 'But' room comes from the 'wee but and ben', the original small croft-house with only two floor-level rooms. The but is the living room and the ben the bedroom. Shetlanders use the words but and ben when referring to the two downstairs rooms in any croft-house.

Chapter 7 Blessings of Home

1 John 14.2, Revised English Bible.

Chapter 12 The Whole Earth Sings

1 The quote about rosaries turning gold is from Janice Connell, *Meetings with Mary: Visions of the Blessed Mother*, Ballantine, 1995.

Chapter 14   Freedom's Song

1 *The New English Hymnal,* The Canterbury Press, 1998.
2 Siegfried Sassoon, 'Everyone Sang', in *The New Golden Treasury of English Verse*, ed. Edward Leesing, Pan, 1980.